The First Week with My New PC

A Very Basic Guide
for Mature Adults and
Everyone Else
Who Wants to
Get Connected

Pamela R. Lessing

Capital Books, Inc.
Sterling, Virginia

Capital Books, Inc.
P.O. Box 605
Herndon, Virginia 20172-0605

Notice of Liability

Trademarks

ISBN 1-892123-22-3   (alk. paper)

Library of Congress Cataloging-in-Publication Data

Lessing, Pamela R.
    The first week with my new PC : a very basic guide for mature adults and everyone who wants to "get connected" / by Pamela R. Lessing.
    p. cm.
Includes index,
ISBN 1-892123-22-3 (alk.)
1. Microcomputers. 2. Computer networks. 3. World Wide Web. I. Title.

QA76.5 L483 2000
004.16--dc21

Book design by Ellen Banker

Printed in Canada on acid-free paper that meets the American National Standards Institute Z39-48 Standard.

First Edition

10 9 8 7 6 5 4 3 2 1

To My Mother

Who, at 85 years of age,
continues to accept challenges
and to be an inspiration to us all.

Contents

Acknowledgments

A book like this would not exist without the help, encouragement, humor, and understanding of family, friends, and business associates. I wish to thank my publisher, Kathleen Hughes of Capital Books, for her immediate interest and enthusiasm. Her knowledge, experience, and versatility make it a pleasure to know her professionally and personally. Without my dear friend Charlotte Gollobin, I never would have met Kathleen. I am grateful to her for her involvement and caring. I am pleased to have worked with David Shenton, my friend and illustrator, who has skillfully combined my thoughts and humor with his creativity and wit to truly enhance this book. In addition, I wish to thank Laurie Harper, my agent, who provided valuable insights and encouragement for this and future projects.

As soon as they heard of this book, many of my friends added their own stories, jokes, and exasperation concerning computers. In particular I have drawn from the joys and difficulties of Ann Kelly, Jane Patton, Maryann Abeles, Betsy Friess, Susan Carabello, Robin Pack, Marsha Caplan, Ellen Landau, P. Bear, and Susan Strauss. In addition, it was Chuck Palmer who managed to explain the unexplainable when I needed clarification myself. I thank these and my many other friends, including Jim Garrett, whose support and understanding meant a great deal to me.

It is to all three generations of my family that I owe particular thanks. My mother was the catalyst for this book, and my greatest pleasure has been her unbridled pride and excitement throughout this project. My sister, Joan, spent almost as much time on the telephone with our mother as I did as she tried to help Mother find lost e-mail, close unwanted windows, and reconnect peripherals. Her good humor, assistance, and understanding carried us through some unusual situations. All of the children contributed to this project with their advice and enthusiasm. Beth was the first to encourage her grandmother to buy a computer, and she was there as her teacher from the beginning. Paul was my advisor, by example, on the Internet. Johan and Anne were supportive of my need to write even during their brief visit. David and Raoul, the "reel" writers in the family, encouraged me with great interest and good questions from the first draft to the final edit.

Finally, I wish to thank Judith. Her persistence, dedication, and advice expanded this project from a helpful guide to a published book. Her technical and editorial skills were only surpassed by her patience and her insights. No one could have shown as much enthusiasm, caring, and support, and I greatly appreciate all that she did.

Introduction
Read This to Find Hidden Special Offer!

Let's be honest. Most people do not read introductions—especially if it is an informational book and all they want to know is how to do some task. In fact I would guess that most people who buy this book will jump ahead to a chapter heading that looks interesting and just "go for it!" This is in spite of the fact that I have gone to a great deal of trouble to lay out a narrative that follows a simple, logical pathway for working with your new computer. That is fine. I am not offended. I personally never read introductions until I am halfway through the book and realize that there might be some useful information at the beginning of the book that will clarify all these other pages. With that in mind, I shall try to offer an introduction that resembles a good newspaper article and provides answers to the questions: who, what, when, where, why?

Who Is This Book For?

This book is written for my mother and for everyone else, whether they have ever touched a computer or not. It is written for you. You pretend that you will never need to learn how to use computers. You have not grown up with computers, and you are really afraid of the machines. You are also embarrassed that you are not a "computer literate" person. However, what is more important is that you are well-read, have some extra time (and money), have an interest in all that is happening around you, and want to keep in touch.

The problem is that you have heard horror stories of computers "crashing," "viruses," documents "lost" for a variety of reasons, and hours of work gone, etc. etc. You have been told, *incorrectly*, that computers are "much too complicated." Or someone has said, "Why do you want to start learning (playing with) something like this now?"

The answer is, "Why Not???" And as for all the things that can go wrong—this guide will help you learn the techniques to prevent disasters. In truth it is most unlikely you will ever be doing work that is so complicated as to have these things happen. (If you get to this level, you will know how to prevent the problems or have the telephone number for tech support on your speed dial.)

What Will I Learn from This Guide?

Everyone learns in a different way. Also, everyone finds one technique that works best for him or her. **This guide will show you a number of different ways to get your computer to do the things you would like it to do.** It will give you a nice narrative in the beginning, along with helpful tips. More importantly, you will have a simple "one, two, three" guide in the back of the book. This will give you several pages of step-by-step instructions that can be a "quick reference" guide. After all, you cannot be expected to remember all the steps after just doing something a few times. Think of it this way: Important businesses and large corporations have used Chapter 11 to get themselves out of trouble for years. Now you have your very own Chapter 11 to bail you out! (There are also appendices full of helpful information.)

When Can I Start? *or*
When Will I Find the Time?

These are two different questions. You can start anytime you want. You might even find this book amusing to read even if you are not sure you want to buy a computer now or ever. In fact, looking over this guide might help you decide whether this is a challenge you really want to try. My own feeling is obvious. I would not have gotten my 85-year-old mother a computer if I had not thought she would be able to manage it and enjoy it. In addition I would not have gone to the trouble of writing this guide if I did not think that this is a skill that anyone can master at any age.

The second question is a bit more difficult. As I point out in Chapter 7, **you will have to practice**. In some ways this is like the piano (but much more interesting)!

In the beginning it will seem to take a great deal of your time. But after a few days, you will find that you are enjoying the time spent on the computer. The Internet will open a whole world of possibilities and it will be fun to send e-mail to friends and family. Still another advantage of taking time each day to "work" on the computer is that it will improve your hand-eye coordination, improve physical dexterity, prevent arthritis from setting in, and keep your mind active. What a deal!

Where Can I Put It?

You no longer need to buy a laptop computer in order to save space. Desktop computers now come with very small towers (the main computer "box") and you can also purchase flat, thin monitors. Space is really not an issue. Think of all the ways you are saving space: You will no longer need a bookshelf full of encyclopedias, reference books, atlases, and telephone directories. You do not even have to keep the local newspaper in order to get the movie listing! (Of course your bookshelf might instead be loaded with computer books like this one!)

Why Should I Be Doing This?

What a silly question! Why shouldn't you be involved with the most interesting communication source that has ever existed? Why shouldn't you be able to get information on any topic that interests you? Think of all the advances that have taken place in your life. While it may have taken you a bit of time to get used to them or know how best to use them, the fact is that you probably do enjoy the remote control for the television, the answering machine for the telephone (not to mention the push-button telephone itself, depending on your age), and many other things that have become a part of your daily life. Age and technical ability are not the issue. Interest and curiosity are!

So now I have gone through the five "Ws", and you are wondering what the "hidden special offer" is. I know that it is difficult to get started and you may not feel comfortable sending your first few e-mail messages. Therefore I am offering to answer one e-mail that I receive from you so that you can test your skills. My address is:

prlessing@bigfoot.com. I might even send you a terrific joke in addition to responding to your message. Of course if you want to send me nice comments about the book, it will make me very happy. However, I shall be happy to hear anything you might like to tell me. Perhaps your suggestion might even be included in the next edition!

Here's a list of activities that you should plan on doing during the first week or two with your new computer:

- Send and receive e-mail.
- Search for something on the World Wide Web.
- Play lots of games like solitaire.
- Use a program (such as the Encarta Encyclopedia) that's on a CD (compact disk) or just listen to an audio CD.
- Write a letter or document of some kind, save what you have written, and print it.

Please *do not panic* after reading this list. The whole point of this guide is to show you the basic, simple way to do all of these things. So let's get started!

1

Chapter One

Out of the Box:
What You Should Do
Whether Help *Is* or *Is Not*
on the Way

I know you are excited because the new
computer has just arrived. You cannot wait to
get *"connected"*—send and receive e-mail,
communicate with the grandchildren at
school, "surf the Web," check your
investments every 15 minutes, etc.
Maybe you have a computer because
your friends all said it was so much fun
playing games and keeping all the
correspondence organized. Whatever the reason, this is *important*:

If you have a child, grandchild, friend, or young neighbor who has offered to help you to set up your new computer, WAIT FOR HIM OR HER TO COME OVER. DO NOT TOUCH ANYTHING!! You have already waited this long—what is a few more hours or days? You can do other things in the meantime like:

- Stock the refrigerator with soda and assorted munchies that this helpful person will appreciate;

- Clear a space where all the new equipment will go. (If you do not have room on a desk, you can buy a special "computer table" for very little money. It will hold everything and there are many different styles.)

- Make sure that an electrical outlet and a phone jack are nearby. If they're not you can go out and buy an extension cord for the telephone—and while you are at it, get a "surge protector" for the computer. Just ask—the salesperson at the computer store or the local hardware store will know what it is.

If you *must* open the box, KEEP EVERYTHING TOGETHER and DO NOT THROW **ANYTHING** OUT (including the box).

Now that you have opened the box, check to see if you have a "printer cable" to connect the printer to the computer. These things are like batteries—they are not included! You will need a printer cable so this is also something you can pick up at your local computer store. The only thing you may take out of the box is the keyboard—this will be explained at the end of this chapter.

Whatever you are thinking, please follow these instructions—they really will save your helper time in the long run, I promise!

If you *do not* have someone to help you, then you should open the box and:

1. Check the list of things to do while you're waiting (above), as it will be good advice for you also (especially the part about food and drink, although your favorites might be stronger than sodas!).

2. Check the section above about opening the box. It is important to keep everything together and not to throw anything out!

3. Get out and *read* the quick set-up information that came with your computer. They really do a great job of explaining where to connect each item and how to get started. *Or go to Chapter 11, where this is explained in detail.*

When everything is connected and the computer is turned on, the first thing you will want to do is make everything easier to see and use. To do this:

1. Press the Windows key (it looks like a flag and is on the bottom line of your keyboard). The "Start" menu will appear. (See figure 1.1.)

2. Press the "S" key. The word "Settings" will be highlighted.

3. Press the "C" key. The control panel will appear. (See figure 1.2.)

4. On the control panel you will see different things that can be set to your preferences. If you go to the picture of a mouse (by moving the mouse in your hand so that the cursor, the thing that looks like an arrow, is sitting on the picture) and then press the left mouse button twice (double-click), a box will appear that gives you a chance to change the settings that are standard. Follow the directions to change settings for mouse speed, to see a tracer showing where the cursor is, or even to change the symbol of the cursor.

5. Also note on the control panel that there is an "icon," or picture, of the standard handicapped symbol. Press the left mouse button twice on this for additional settings that might help you.

6. *Go to Chapter 11 where all this is explained in detail.*

7. Consider hiring someone to come over and set up all the basics that are described in the next chapter! It is worth the money!

Figure 1.1

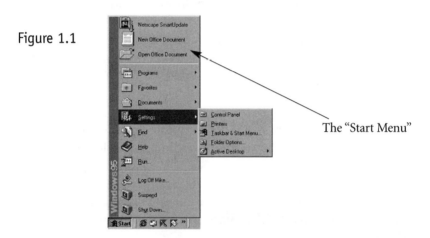

The "Start Menu"

Figure 1.2

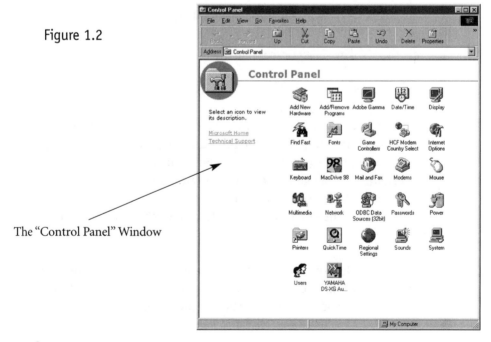

The "Control Panel" Window

The Keyboard

If you are used to using a typewriter, then a number of things on your new computer keyboard will look familiar. However, some of the keys work differently than they do on your old typewriter. So even if they do look similar, you will need to learn to use them in other ways.

An example is the "Enter" key, which is in the same position and looks like the "return" key on your typewriter. On the typewriter this key would move the carriage over, allowing you to type the next line of text. On the computer it is different, as the words "wrap around" or drop to the next line automatically and you do not have to tell the machine to start a new line of text. The "Enter" key on the computer does drop your text down one line (for example, when you want to start a new paragraph). However, it also can act like a shortcut or command for the computer. Pressing this key is like saying "go find" when you have typed in a Web address. It is also like saying "OK" or "show me this" when you have identified or "highlighted" something that you want to do. (See figure 1.3.)

Figure 1.3 The Keyboard

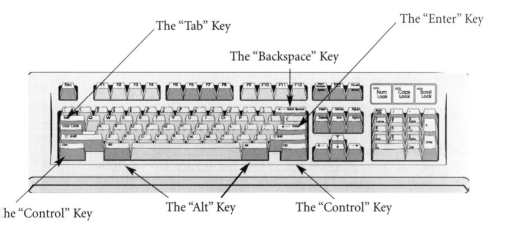

Everything will be much clearer when you have some idea of where different keys are and what some of the new keys are called. Some examples:

- Find the key that has "Ctrl" on it. This is the "Control" key. There are two of them. There is no difference between the two. Use the key that is most convenient for you. It is usually as easy as deciding which hand is closest to a "Control" key when you need to press one. The "Control" key is used as a shortcut for a variety of tasks; for a list of shortcuts, see Appendix B.

- Find the key that has "Alt" on it. This is the "Alternate" key. There may be two of them depending on your keyboard. Again it is just a question of convenience.

- Between the "Alt" key and the "Ctrl" key is a key that looks like a flag. It is the "Windows" key. This is the key that will bring up the "Start" menu, and it is meant to look like the symbol for Microsoft® Windows®. There are two of these keys and they respond the same way, but the positioning is different.

- Check where the "Tab" key is as you will be using this a lot.

- You will also be using the "Enter" key, the "Backspace" key, and the keys to the right of the main keyboard that have "arrows" on them.

If you have trouble finding these different keys, go ahead and look at Figure 1.3 on page 9. I know there are lots of other new keys that you are wondering about, but you will not need them right away. This guide is to help you with your early days on the computer. So very simply put, if I do not mention it in this book, DON'T TOUCH IT YET!

2

Chapter Two
Everything Is Connected
So Now What Do I Do?

So the computer is sitting in front of you and if you have a wonderful helper, he or she has raced through all the steps to "install" whatever they think you need. In addition they have probably been really efficient and registered all your new equipment. If you do not have anyone to help, this is not a problem. There are detailed instructions in this book as to how to do all of the things mentioned below. Just turn to Chapter 11 and get started.

Here are some things that you will need to know and do. If you have a helper who is *really* nice, please ask him or her to:

- Show you how to turn the computer on and how to shut it off (see end of chapter);

- Show you where and how to put CDs and floppy disks into the tower;

- Slow down the mouse, add a "trail" so you can see where it is moving, and enlarge the size of the "cursor";

Figure 2.1

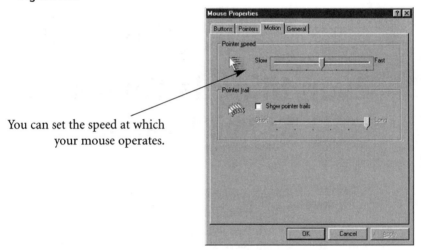

You can set the speed at which your mouse operates.

- Get you signed on with an Internet Service Provider (ISP) and help you pick out your user name and password;

- Set up an "address book" with all the e-mail addresses of family and friends. (Also ask them to put together a "buddy list" while you have them here and happily working for you!);

- Make sure you have a "folder" on your "desktop" that is called "My Documents." Also have them add into that folder several other new folders with names like "Correspondence," "House," "Car," etc. (Don't forget to have folders with the names of all your kids and that favorite grandchild who is helping you put all this together!);

- Show you how to open, move, resize, and close windows;

- Set up a "template" with your letterhead and a fax letterhead. (If they really know what they are doing and have the time, or are willing to come back, which might depend on whether you have good snacks.) They can then also set up which "font" and what color lettering you would like to use for all your correspondence;

- Put the shortcuts for your Internet Service Provider, your letterhead, and a few games like solitaire on your desktop; and

- Make sure all written work is automatically saved to "My Documents" as a "default" so that none of your work is lost.

If you do not have a wonderful, helpful person with you, DO NOT PANIC! Go to Chapter 11 for all the information on how to do these things. Also do not panic that you do not know the meanings of lots of the terms I have just used, like "default" and "fonts." They are really unimportant for right now and were only mentioned with the thought that you might have a person sitting there ready to help you get started. (However, this is a good time to mention that you should keep a notebook by the computer so you can write down any questions you have. Some of your questions may be answered in the back of this book, but some may not. By writing things down, you can ask someone for help or perhaps e-mail the question to a friend or to me. That way I will know what I have left out and need to add in the next edition!)

A term that you *do* have to know is "*desktop.*" The screen in front of you looks like a television, but is usually called a "monitor." Where you normally see only one big picture on your television, your desktop has lots of little pictures of things or "icons." You will also have several things that my mother calls "frames" and that the industry calls "windows." (See figure 2.2.)

Try to think of the screen in front of you as the desk at which you sit in your office or study. On your desk you have your telephone to the right and your address book next to it. On the left you might have a box with bills that need to be paid or a folder with letters to be answered. You leave the middle area of your desk clear so that you have a place to do your work.

The screen in front of you is just like the desk at which you sit. It is called the "desktop." On the desktop you have different things that you can work on, or play with, that are depicted as "icons" or pictures on the left side. In the middle area you have a place on which to do your work as soon as you have opened up these folders or games. So how do you open these folders and start to work or play? That question is answered in the next chapter!

Figure 2.2 The Desktop

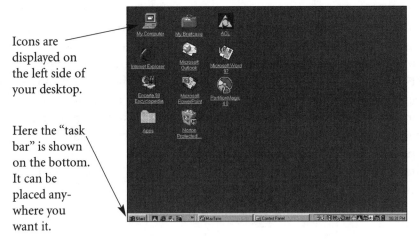

Icons are displayed on the left side of your desktop.

Here the "task bar" is shown on the bottom. It can be placed anywhere you want it.

Some Thoughts on Turning the Computer On and Turning the Computer Off

Computers operate differently from other electrical equipment. You do not need to "shut down" the computer every night. It is not like the television, the iron, the coffeemaker, or the air-conditioner. It will not blow up, burn out, use too much electricity, or hurt anything. The machine is designed to "stay on." (If you go away for several days, it is a good idea to turn it off. However, it can stay on day after day just waiting for you to come and play with it!) The step-by-step guide for turning the computer on, turning it off, and restarting it is in Chapter 11 beginning on page 91.

3

Chapter Three
The First Time:
All Alone with the Computer
(Will My Family Still Respect
Me in the Morning?)

This is that special moment. You are
excited, but also a little anxious. Maybe you
have read some books on the subject, or
maybe you thought it would be better
just to experience everything as it comes.
(Well, I guess the latter can't be true if
you are reading this, but you know what I
mean!) You might also be thinking that this is
the worst moment in your life. How could you
be so stupid as to spend this amount of money
on something you will never figure out.

The *most important* fact you need to know is that you cannot break anything by just pushing some of the keys. You may open up a whole lot of windows that you do not want; you may have everything "freeze" (nothing seems to work—mouse, keys, etc.); or everything may go blank as the whole thing "crashes."

BUT, DO NOT WORRY! First of all, you have not put any important information into the computer, so you have nothing that can be lost. Also, if all else fails, you can just turn off the computer with the button on the PC or "tower." (It is that rectangular box that does not look like a television, but is connected to everything else and is the "brains" of all this.) That allows you to restart the computer and just try again. You may get a nasty message from the computer that you did not shut it down properly, but you are all alone, so you are the only one that knows you made it unhappy. Anyway, it is a machine and you are the boss. (Although it should be noted that it will act like a two-year-old and refuse to do things at times because it says that it can't. But, unlike a two-year-old, it is telling the truth and you may need to stop and figure out why it will not do what you want it to do.)

18

This may also be the moment that you wish you had hired some computer expert to come in and give you lessons. To be honest, you will need to have someone give you lessons at one point. However, the idea for this first week is to get you moving with your new computer and not to be overwhelmed by the 13-year-old who is pushing keys faster than the speed of light. It will also give you a chance to figure out what questions you have, so that you do not feel you are wasting time and money when the teacher arrives.

By the way, this may be a good time to mention that I suggest that you *do not* give your computer a name. It will only empower the machine in your mind, and your family and friends may become jealous when you start spending all your time with Jim or Judith and speak of him or her with greater affection than you ever did any of them.

Before we *really* get started, you will need to understand some terms and try to practice a few of the techniques or moves that you will need to get the computer to do what you want. Please understand that there are several ways of doing the same task. It is similar to skiing in that there are always several ways to come down the mountain. (Even an expert skier likes to take easier trails or shortcuts sometimes.) Some people will find all the techniques easy and others will need to try alternate approaches. Some people find it easy to move the mouse all over the desktop and think this is better than remembering "commands" or special keys to press. Others may have trouble using the mouse because they have arthritis or tremors, or have a hard time seeing where they are pointing the "cursor."

Once you have tried several methods you will know which one is best for you. In order to make this book easier for you to use, I shall give the instructions for using both the mouse and the keyboard commands to perform different tasks. Each method will be clearly labeled. This means that if you know you want to use keyboard commands, you can skip the paragraph that gives instructions on how to use the mouse to perform a task and vice versa.

Using the Mouse

So the first thing is to take the mouse in your hand—left or right, it makes no difference (see "The Mouse for Lefties" at the end of the chapter). The only thing that is important is that the "tail" (or cord) is pointed away from you or "up." Now just move the mouse around and see where the cursor goes.

The cursor will look like an arrow, large letter "I," or hand, depending on where it is on the desktop or in an open window. Don't worry. The different looks are signs to you that the cursor can do different things. For example, when you are working with text, the cursor can be your "insertion" point. If you want to add a word or phrase in the middle of a line, you place the cursor at the spot where you want to begin. Then you press the left mouse button once (click). There is now a blinking "I" in that spot and it shows that this is where the words will appear when you start typing. More on this later! (See figure 3.1.)

Figure 3.1

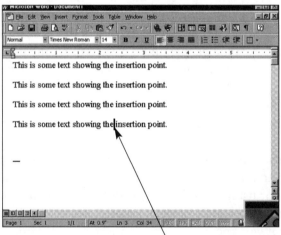

You can insert a word or a phrase here by placing your cursor at the spot where you want to begin.

Notice that you do not need to stretch your arm all the way to the kitchen to move the cursor to the far corner of the computer desktop. If you are near the edge of the mouse pad, but the cursor is not yet over to that icon in the upper right-hand corner, physically pick up the mouse and place it back in the middle of the mouse pad. Then start moving it again. (Go ahead and try this now. You see, it is the ball under this contraption that is causing the cursor to move. When it is not in motion, nothing happens. Hold the mouse in one hand and place your other hand on the ball on its underside. With your finger, roll the ball around and look at the monitor to see where the cursor is moving.)

Your hand should be holding the mouse lightly and you should be comfortable. You should also be able to reach the left and right buttons at the top of the mouse with your index and middle fingers. Now *this is important:* For the next few weeks *do not* press (click) the *right* mouse button. YOU DO NOT NEED IT IN THE BEGINNING.

Opening and Closing Windows

Practice "clicking" or pressing the *left* mouse button by pointing the cursor (the arrow, hand, large "I") on an icon and pressing the left button once (clicking) or twice ("double-clicking"—two rapid clicks). Then relax your death grip on the mouse! If everything is lined up correctly you will have just opened *something.* It really does not matter what.

Figure 3.2

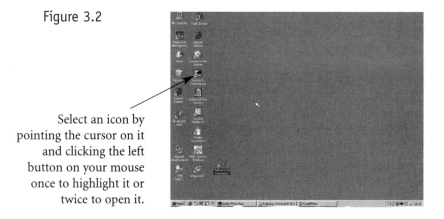

Select an icon by pointing the cursor on it and clicking the left button on your mouse once to highlight it or twice to open it.

The reason it does not matter is that you will also learn how to "close" that window since you do not need it for this exercise. Whatever has just opened has a blue line running along the top of the window that shows that it is "active"—that you are working with it. This line is called the "title bar." It is important to remember that name, as your grandchild (or friendly helper) may refer to it when giving you instructions over the telephone. At the extreme right side of the title bar (the blue line) are three little squares. One of the squares has an "X" in it (it is the one all the way to the right). Point the cursor at the "X" inside this box and press (click) on the *left* mouse button once. (See figure 3.3.)

Figure 3.3

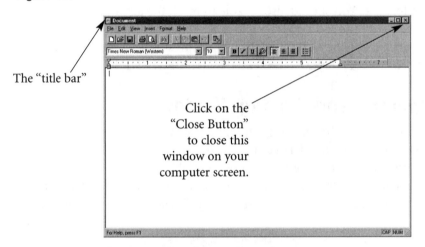

The "title bar"

Click on the
"Close Button"
to close this
window on your
computer screen.

Now the window is gone! Knowing how to open and close windows is probably one of the most important lessons you will learn, so just practice this a few times. (My mother refers to closing the window as "X-ing it out.") Another way to close any window is to press the "ctrl" key and the "F4" key simultaneously. These keys magically get you out of things you do not want. (Wouldn't it be great to have something like this in our everyday lives?)

Finding Help

The other thing you may have noticed is that as you move the cursor around an open window, or as you put the point of the cursor on the "X" to close the window, a little box drops down. This box gives you an explanation of what will happen if you press the left mouse button (click) on that icon (picture). This is a big help as you do not need to remember what every icon means or how every icon is used right now. When you use the computer, you will start to remember where an icon is placed and what it does, but you will always have this backup if you forget.

Another way to get help is from the "Help" menu that comes with every program. It sits with other words, not icons, in a gray, rectangular box just below the title bar (that blue line that shows an active window). This line is called the "menu bar."

You can open this menu, and others, in three ways.

Mouse Commands: Point the cursor at the word "Help" and press the left mouse button once while it is pointed at that word. A "menu" of various choices will drop down. Pressing the left mouse button (clicking) on the highlighted "Help" item will cause a whole list of topics to appear.

Just press on the left mouse button once (click) on the thing you want to know more about, and the information will appear. To get to the item you want you can use the arrow keys on the right side of the keyboard to scroll down, or you can type in a keyword in the space provided. In either case you then press the "Enter" key and that will give you helpful information.

Keyboard Commands: Another way to get a "Help" menu is to press the "Alt" key and hold it down while you press the "H" key (Alt+H). (Important: Whenever you hold keys down simultaneously, you must let go right away or the machine will make "binging" sounds or start answering commands you did not even know you were giving. Please remember that you only need a *quick, light* touch on the mouse and the keyboard.)

F1 Key: The last way to get a "Help" menu is to go to the top of your keyboard on the left side. There you will see keys that are labeled "F1," "F2," "F3," etc. The first key—"F1" also says "Help" on it, and by pressing this key you will get a "Help" menu. *Caution:* Please do not press any of the extra buttons you see on the keyboard right now, just the ones mentioned here.

Menus and Other Shortcuts

That brings us to another way to move around the desktop without using the mouse. These are shortcuts and commands that are not just for the arthritic, but are used by the experts to get things done quickly.

Look at Figure 3.4 below. You see an open window on the desktop. At the top is the name of the program you are using, or the folder that is open. (Remember this is shown as white letters on a blue line and is called the title bar.) Below that you have one or more gray lines. One gray line will have icons and the other will have words. Look at the line with the words. This is the menu bar. It is from these menus that you can ask the computer to do some task like printing your work, saving a note into a specific folder, changing the size and font of a document, etc.

Figure 3.4

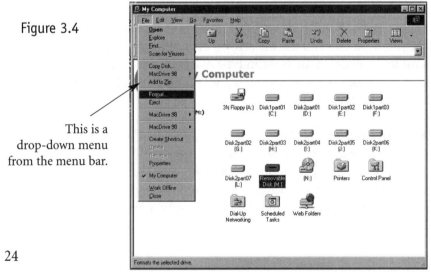

This is a drop-down menu from the menu bar.

So, how do you get the menu to drop down and give you choices? Notice that one letter in each word on the menu bar is underlined. In the word "File" it is the "F" and in the word "Edit" it is the "E." These words are lead-ins to menus. To open a menu, press the "Alt" key and hold it down while you press down the underlined key of the menu you want to see (example: press Alt+F). Then release both keys. Now you have a menu with a lot of possibilities—words and commands that are written in black. (You will also see some words that are written in gray, not black. They are "shaded" and hard to read. These are choices that are not available to you at this time. More on this later.)

Once again, all the words on the menu will have one letter that is underlined. If you want the computer to "Save" or "Print" or "Exit" you just press the letter "S" or "P" or "X" or whatever the underlined letter is. Then another box will appear that will ask you a few questions in order to complete your request/command. This is a dialog box. If you pressed the "X" key it is telling the computer that you want to close this program. It is like pressing the left mouse button (clicking) on the "X" in the little box on the top right of your window.

As an example, if you are playing a card game like Free Cell, you would start by pointing the cursor on the Free Cell icon on the desktop and pressing the left mouse button twice (double-clicking). Then you would have a window open on the desktop that would show a green playing area. Now what?!

Notice that there is a menu bar, a gray line with two words on it— "Game" and "Help"—and the "G" and "H" are underlined. If you press the "Alt" key and the "G" key simultaneously (Alt+G) a menu appears, and if you now press the "N" key, the cards for the next game will be dealt. If you want to know how to play the game, press the "Alt" key and the "H" key (Alt+H) and bring up the "Help" menu. (See figure 3.5.) *A list of the most important "Control" and "Alt" key shortcuts and commands are listed in Appendix B.*

Figure 3.5

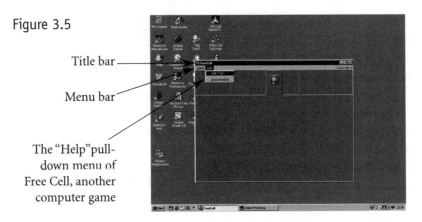

Title bar

Menu bar

The "Help" pull-
down menu of
Free Cell, another
computer game

So now you know how to open a menu, but maybe the words in the menu are a bit difficult to read or you are not sure what letter is underlined. This is the moment when you use the arrow keys. With the menu open, tap the arrow keys up, down, right, or left to highlight a different word or command. When you have the word you want highlighted, press the "Enter" key to say, "OK, do this." (Think of the remote control for your television. When you press "Enter" it is like saying, "Yes, I want this channel.")

The arrow keys are useful for many things. They can move the cursor to different spots on a letter or document that you are writing. They can also "scroll" (move) down a section of the e-mail that you are reading. That way you do not have to hold down the mouse button on the arrow symbol at the bottom of the scroll bar. (The scroll bar is a vertical bar on the right or a horizontal bar on the bottom of an open window. It is active when a window is too small to show all the available information. By clicking on the appropriate arrow, more data is visible. For scroll bars see Figure 9.1. Also see Chapter 11.)

Arrow keys can also help you "highlight" a word, sentence, or page of text. All you need to do is use the arrow key to move the cursor to the beginning of the word/sentence/page to be highlighted. Then hold down the "Shift" key and use the arrow key to move the cursor to the end of the word/sentence/page. Finish by releasing the "Shift" key. Now that area is highlighted, and there are all sorts of things you can do with a highlighted area! Note: You can also lose the highlighted area if you are not careful. So *be careful.* **DO NOT** press "Backspace" or "Delete." (See *"Undoing" the Damage* at the end of the chapter.)

The last technique you need to practice is called "dragging." By now you are probably bored with all this and just want to do something *real* with your computer. That is fine. You can learn to "click and drag" some other time. Just remember that it is something you will definitely need in the near future so note that Chapter 7 describes this technique.

The Mouse for Lefties

One can change the mouse for use by left-handed people. Open the "Start" menu by pressing the Windows key (the one that looks like a flag, second from the left on the bottom row of the keyboard). Press the up arrow key and go to "Settings." Use the right arrow key to open the next menu where the word "Control Panel" should be highlighted. Press the "Enter" key. In the control panel window, find the mouse icon; point the cursor on it and press the left mouse button twice (double-click). In the dialog box "Mouse Properties," point the cursor on the "Buttons" tab and press the left mouse button once (click). Choose the option that you want ("left-handed") by pressing the "L" key. Finish by pointing the cursor on the "OK" button and clicking. Close the window by pointing the cursor on the "X" on the right side of the title bar (blue bar at the top of the window) and clicking. *Please*

Figure 3.6

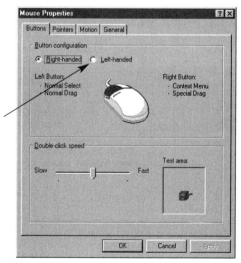

From the Mouse Properties dialog box you can change the button configuration of your mouse so left-handed users can use the right mouse button (with index finger) for normal select and normal drag.

27

note: if you make this change, every time I tell you to press the left mouse button, you need to press the *right* mouse button.

"Undoing" the Damage

There are two remedies if you make a mistake, but you must *immediately* correct your mistake.

Keyboard Commands: Do you see the word "Edit" on the menu bar? Press the "Alt" key and the "E" key (Alt+E) to drop down this menu or point the cursor on the word "Edit" and press the left mouse button once (click). Press the letter "U" or highlight the word "Undo" at the top of the menu. Press the "Enter" key. Everything is now back the way it was. (The key command for this is the "Control" key plus the "Z" key (Ctrl+Z).

Mouse Commands: If you prefer using the icon bar, find the fourth rectangle from the left. The icon looks like an arrow curving backwards and that is what it means—"go back to the way things were!" Point the cursor at this icon and press the left mouse button once (click).

Both of these approaches result in the "Undo" command. "Undo" is one of the most important commands that you will ever use. It will:

• Correct the mistake you just made.

• Take you back to whatever was on your page originally if, after making a correction or change in formatting, you now decide you do not want that paragraph to be bold, italicized or underlined.

• If you make a mess editing your work or you are now three pages off because your cat walked across the keyboard, it will take everything back to the original.

Don't you wish we could do this in real life?

4

Chapter Four
What Is the Internet?
What Is a "User Name"?
Just Tell Me How to Find Out What the Weather Will Be *HERE*!

So everyone is talking about the Internet. Every television show, magazine, and advertisement directs you to the "World Wide Web" and offers you "information."

Your question is, "How does this work and what does it mean to me?"

The Internet is a series of interconnected computer systems and services that is worldwide.

Try to think of the Internet as our country. In our country there are cities, and in each city there are buildings. Each city has a different function or job. One city just handles commercial affairs and so it is given an address or name that is ".com." Another city is responsible for all the educational facilities and so its name is ".edu." Still other cities have names like ".net," ".org," ".gov," etc., and each one of these names stand for the type of thing that the city does.

Within each city there are buildings and each one of these is the name of a particular company, school, organization, or network. This is also called the "domain name."

For example, one of the better-known U.S. government agencies is the National Oceanographic and Atmospheric Administration. It issues weather reports along with lots of other interesting information. It is a part of the government of the United States so its Internet address is: www.noaa.gov. A college will have an address that is the name of the school followed by ".edu "; Ithaca College is www.ithaca.edu. National Public Radio, a non-profit organization, can be reached at www.npr.org. A popular commercial address is www.barnesandnoble.com, the online store bookseller.

Now within each "building" there are individuals or areas that you will want to contact. After all, you really do not want to communicate with just anyone at National Public Radio, or Ithaca College, or NOAA and the Department of Commerce. The "user name" refers to the specific person or area that you want to go to inside this "building."

As an example, your grandchild named Joan gets her "e-mail" (electronic mail) from the server called "Juno." This company lives in a "building" called juno.com and your grandchild has decided to use her initials as her user name. Her e-mail address would then be jcl@juno.com. (The "@" sign means "at.") If e-mail is sent from one individual in a "building" to someone in the same "building," it is not necessary to put in the name of the "building," (Internet Service Provider). You only need to put the user name in the "Send To" box. Think of it this way: The manager of your "building" knows everyone who lives and works in the building. He does not need to be told that Jane, David, Raoul, or Betsy live there. He only needs to know that you want to send your message to Jane, or to David and Raoul, or to Betsy. (You can also send it to all of them at once!)

Now perhaps you would like to try to use the Internet to find something useful such as the movies that are playing in your area. If you use America Online (AOL) as your Internet Service Provider (ISP), the easiest way to get this information is to "sign on" to AOL. Then go to the fourth line down from the top of the window. Look for the box that says, "Type Keyword or Web Address Here." (It is just below the line with lots of icons in colored rectangles. See Figure 4.1.) Type in the word "movies" or www.bouldermovies.com. (I have used my hometown as the example. You need to type in the name of your city and then the word "movies" followed by ".com.") Detailed instructions on how to do all this are in Chapter 11.

Figure 4.1

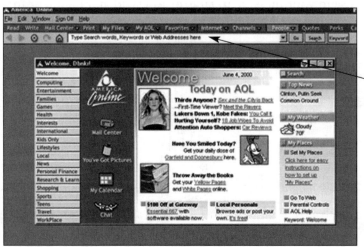

You may type in a keyword to get in-depth information on a subject, or type in a Web address to go to a Web site right from the Welcome screen.

You also might want to know how to get the weather for today in your own area or anywhere in the world. If you use America Online as your ISP, whenever you "sign on" there will be a window in front of you that will offer all sorts of instant information (along with telling you if you have received any e-mail from your best friend!). If you point the cursor on the spot that says "Weather" and press once on the left mouse button (click), it will give you a complete forecast for your area.

If you want to know the weather in some other part of the country or the world, you can go to the fourth line down from the top of the window. Look for the box that says "Type Keyword or Web Address Here." (It is just below the line with lots of icons in colored rectangles.) Type in the word "weather" or www.noaa.gov or www.weather.com. Then press the "Enter" key. (You have probably figured this out, but "www" stands for World Wide Web and *usually* needs to go in front of the Internet address.)

In any case, always type in the "address" exactly as it was given to you. YOU MUST BE PRECISE! DO NOT ADD SPACES. DO PLACE PERIODS (.) AND FORWARD SLASHES (/) EXACTLY AS DIRECTED. If you do not, the computer gets very unhappy and will refuse to take you to the Web site that you want to reach.

5

Chapter Five
The Time Has Come:
I Am Really Ready to
DO SOMETHING

First Question: What is it that *you* would most like to do with this computer?

For most people the answer is that they want to know how to send and receive e-mail. Creating and printing out documents is usually less of a priority. After all, you can still write letters by hand. Assuming that you, or your helpful young person, have set up an account or "trial account" with one of the Internet Service Providers (ISP) like America Online, Juno, ATT, or Microsoft Network, you can get started very easily. (If this is still to be done, see **Setting Up an ISP Account** at the end of this chapter.)

For convenience, I shall use America Online (AOL), version 5.0, as the example when describing all the different ways to use e-mail and to connect to the World Wide Web. I do this for a number of reasons, but not in any way to endorse one service over another. Remember that each of the Internet Service Providers will give you a free trial period. This means that you can "sign on" with AOL (or another service) for 100+ hours and get used to doing basic tasks and then try another ISP to see if that one works better for you.

Getting Connected

The first thing you will need to do is tell the computer that you want to work in the program AOL. The way to do this is to "open" it.

There are several ways to do this:

1. The easiest is to point the cursor on the icon that looks like a triangle in a blue box on the left of your desktop. With the cursor on the icon, press the left mouse button twice (double-click). (Remember we are only using the *left* mouse button for now.)

2. Another way to open your ISP is to go to the icon at the top left of your desktop that looks like a computer and says "My Computer" under it. Point the cursor on this icon and double-click on the left mouse button. Now use the right arrow key to move over to and highlight the gray icon that looks like a rectangle and has [C:] under it. Press the "Enter" key. (If you prefer using the mouse, point the cursor on this icon and double-click). (See Figure 5.1.)

Figures 5.1 and 5.2

AOL Icon

My Computer Icon

These are how icons will look on your desktop.

The "C" Drive

You now have all the programs and information on your "C drive" in nice folders in front of you! (DO NOT PANIC! Yes, there are a lot of folders in front of you, but you will only need two folders for the next few weeks.) The folders are placed alphabetically so find the folder that says "AOL" and highlight it either by pointing the cursor on it and pressing the left mouse button once (clicking), or by using the arrow keys to get to it. When that folder is highlighted, press the "Enter" key or press the left mouse button twice (double-click). (See Figure 5.2.)

Great! Now you are looking at more folders and icons. One of the icons will be dark blue with a turquoise triangle in the middle. Under the icon it will say "AOL.exe." You should highlight this icon by moving the arrow keys to get to it and then pressing the "Enter" key. (Alternative: point the cursor at it and double-click.)

Congratulations! You have opened the program that will lead you to the Internet. *You are about to become connected!* Notice that there is a window in the center of your desktop that has a blue line running along the top. The name of the program, "AOL," is in the upper left corner. (Remember: This blue bar is called the title bar. Below that is a gray line with words that correspond to menus that is called the menu bar, and below that are several colored rectangles with lots of icons.)

In the middle of the window is another smaller window that also has a blue line running across the top or title bar. This title bar has the words "Sign On" to the left. If everything has been set up properly, you will see your user name in the center of the window. In addition there might be a rectangle below your user name so that you can enter a password. Enter the password that you have chosen. (You or your help-ful young person can set up your account so that your user name and password run automatically and you do not have to enter this informa-tion every time. However, if you prefer you can go through this process whenever you want to sign on.) Try to make the password a very sim-ple thing, like your birthday or your maiden name, so it is really easy for you to remember. Also make a note of it somewhere, in case you do forget.

Now point the cursor on the blue rectangle in the lower right area and press the left mouse button once (click) on the square labeled "Sign On."

Now WAIT!

CONTINUE TO WAIT.

I MEAN IT, JUST WAIT AS THE MODEM CONNECTS WITH THE ISP.

This can take a bit of time as your computer's modem is dialing up a special telephone number and trying to get recognized. Sometimes the modem will have to dial two numbers before it connects. (Note that the computer uses your telephone line to connect to the Internet. Unless you have a second telephone line, this means that while you are "on-line" you can't make or receive phone calls.)

• Listen to the sounds the modem makes;

• Look over the glossary of terms in the back of this book;

• If you have a second telephone line, call up your children or friends and tell them you are about to send them e-mail if this stupid machine really works; or

• Look at the next diagram, which will prepare you for your "Welcome" window. (See Figure 5.3.)

Reading and Sending E-mail

Once you are connected to AOL, a new window will appear and a voice will say "Welcome." If someone has sent you e-mail the voice will also say the famous line, "You've Got Mail!" If no one has sent you any e-mail, make a note to call all your friends, children, and grandchildren and tell them that you are going to a great deal of trouble, time, and expense to move into the 21st century. You expect them to cooperate (read: humor you) and send some mail with which you can practice! Don't forget to tell them what your e-mail address is (see **Your E-mail Address** at the end of this chapter).

The window looks like the Figure 5.3 and is called the "Welcome" window. There are just one or two things about it that are interesting to notice right now. The most important is to find the thing that looks like a mailbox. It sits inside a blue vertical rectangle on the left side of this new window. If there is a yellow square in it and the red flag is up, this is the sign that you have received e-mail. Move the cursor over to the mailbox icon and press the left mouse button once (click).

Figure 5.3

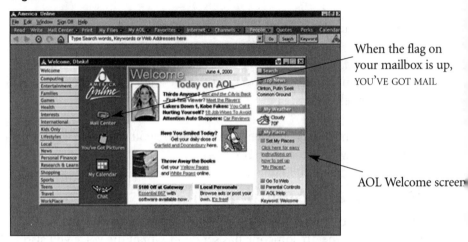

When the flag on your mailbox is up, YOU'VE GOT MAIL

AOL Welcome screen

A new window will open and it will look like Figure 5.4. Notice that the "New Mail" folder in front of you will show a date, a user name, and a subject. The top "piece" of mail will be *highlighted*. To read this e-mail you can either point the cursor on the message and press the left mouse button twice (double-click) or just press the "Enter" key. (Remember the "Enter" key is like saying, "yes, I want this." And yes, there are other ways to read your e-mail, but these two are the easiest for now.)

Figure 5.4

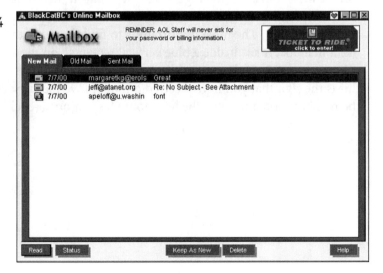

Congratulations again! You are now reading your first e-mail. Now you have to decide what you want to do. You have several choices:

• Reply to the e-mail;

• Read your next message;

• Go and get something to drink—you have accomplished a major task! or

• Call the person who sent you this e-mail and tell them you got it!

The last choice defeats the purpose of having e-mail, but you are excited and it is fine to do this once in the first week. A better idea is to reply to the person, as this will give you practice writing and sending e-mail. It will also show them that you are "computer literate."

It is very easy to reply to the e-mail you have received. Look to the right of the message. (See figure 5.5.). There are several icons in a vertical row. The top one says "Reply," the next says "Forward," and the bottom one says "Add Address." Move the cursor to the icon that says "Reply" and press the left mouse button once (click). You should now have a new window.

Figure 5.5

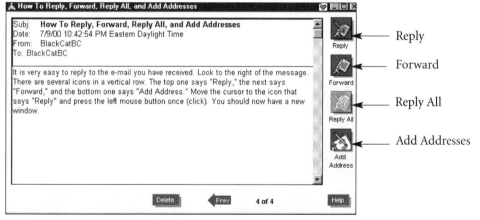

41

This is your "piece of paper" on which to write your return note. Notice that all the work has been done for you. The "Send To" box already has the correct e-mail address. The "Subject" box refers to the subject of the note the person sent to you. The large box below this is the area that you will use to write your note. Best of all, the cursor is already blinking in this box so that all you have to do is start typing your response. (Some people, like my mother, have trouble seeing the blinking cursor. There is a simple test that will show you that the cursor is in the correct spot. Press the space bar several times. You should now see the cursor blinking in the message area.)

You should also note that the icons in the vertical line to the right have now changed. (See figure 5.6.) The choices you now have are "Send Now," "Send Later," and "Address Book." After you type your message, you need to send it to that person. Just writing the message is not enough! Most of the time, the best thing to do is to place the cursor on the "Send Now" icon and press the left mouse button (click).

Figure 5.6

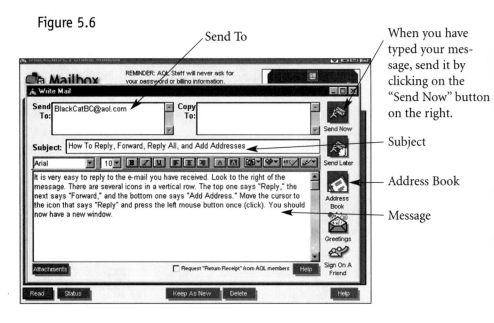

Send To

When you have typed your message, send it by clicking on the "Send Now" button on the right.

Subject

Address Book

Message

If you think that you might want to make some changes to your message you can point the cursor at the "Send Later" icon and click. (I will get back to the address book in a moment.) After you click on the icon, a dialog box will appear that will tell you that your mail has been sent (or that it is waiting to be sent). You *must* respond to this message. In fact whenever the computer asks you a question or tells you something, you *must* respond by moving the cursor to the box and clicking on "OK" or "Cancel." Another way of doing this is by pressing the "Enter" key, or pressing the "Y" for yes or the "N" for no. The computer will not respond to any commands until you have answered its statement or question. (Remember, I told you in Chapter 3 that the machine is sometimes like a two-year-old!)

After you have acknowledged that your outgoing mail has been sent, the original message that was sent to you will appear again. Now you have another choice to make. You might want some friend or family member to read the message that you just received. If that is the case, look at the right vertical icons, place the cursor on the second icon that says "Forward," and press the left mouse button once (click).

The new window in front of you looks different from the one you just used for your reply.(See figure 5.7.) What has just happened? The computer has copied the message that was sent to you and is ready to send this message on to another person or group of people. All you have to do is fill in the "Send To" box and add a brief comment in the message box. (You can also change the "Subject" box.)

It really helps to add a message so that the person to whom you are forwarding this mail knows why you are sending it. A short message like: "Johan and Anne, thought this would amuse you" or "Alex, I never knew she would say such a stupid thing" will indicate that you meant to send this on and that you did not just push the wrong buttons.

Now all you do is move the cursor to "Send Now" or "Send Later" and press the left mouse button once (click). You will not see the message that you have decided to forward. You will only see your additional message. Do not worry, a copy really is forwarded to whomever you indicated.

43

Figure 5.7

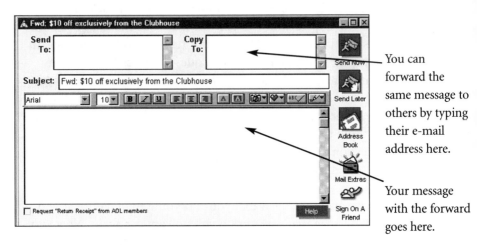

You can forward the same message to others by typing their e-mail address here.

Your message with the forward goes here.

Yes, but how do I send the forward this message (or any message) to my daughter when her address is not already in the "Send To" box?

Good question. The cursor will be blinking in the "Send To" box. Point the cursor on your address book in the vertical icon area to the right and open it by pressing on the left mouse button once (clicking). If you are lucky, the nice person who helped you set up the computer also filled in the e-mail addresses of family and friends. If not, you need to look in Chapter 11 where this procedure is explained in detail.

Look for the name of the person to whom you wish to forward the message. (If you have lots of names, use the arrow key to scroll down the list.) Highlight the name of the correct person and then either press the "Enter" key or point the cursor on the name and double-click.

Look at the "Send To" box. The correct e-mail address is now there. If you want to send the message to more than one person just do the same thing again and another e-mail address will be added to this box.

Now it is time to learn another "trick"!

The easy way to go to the next box is to press the "Tab" key. You have filled in the "Send To" box and you want to fill in the "Subject" box. Press the "Tab" key until the cursor is blinking in that box. Fill in your subject and then press the "Tab" key again. Now the cursor will be blinking in the area where you will write your message! There are other ways to get to each of the boxes—an example is that you can place the cursor in the desired box and press the left mouse button once (click). *However, using the "Tab" key to move around is a very important skill and something that you need to remember.*

Now let me make another point. You do not have to do anything with the e-mail that you have been sent. No one says that you have to answer it. You may want to read it, you may not. You may want to wait to read it at another time, and that is fine. Nothing is going to happen to the mail you have been sent. It does not get lost. It actually goes to a "Mail Center," and it is kept in a file called "Incoming Saved Mail." If you do choose to wait to read it or you wish to reply to it later, it will be there for you.

You can now get your next message. Look at the arrows on the lower right of the message box and, with the cursor on the word "Next" or "Previous," press the left mouse button once (click). Your next piece of e-mail will appear. When you close that message (do this by pointing the cursor on the "X" in the upper right corner and clicking), you will see the "New Mail" list once again. By highlighting another line with the arrow keys and pressing the "Enter" key (or using the mouse), you can now read another e-mail message.

Let me be the first to warn you that you may not want to open and read all the e-mail that is sent to you. Often there will be mail from unknown people or groups that offer sexually explicit photos or fantastic opportunities to buy things. The general rule is that if you do not recognize the user name, do not open the e-mail. Now this might be difficult for you in the beginning as you are unfamiliar with all the "addresses" of family and friends. You can keep a list of addresses near the computer as a reference. Or you can just recognize that in the first few weeks you might wind up opening some mail with unexpected results!

If you want to get rid of unwanted e-mail, the way to do this is to "delete" the message. This is very easy to do. Look at the list of your incoming e-mail and see if you wish to get rid of messages from unknown sources, or old messages that are no longer of interest. Notice that under the message box there are several blue rectangular "buttons"; in the middle there is one labeled "Delete." Point the cursor on this button and press the left mouse button once (click). If you are actively connected to AOL ("signed on") when you do this, the message will be deleted immediately. If you are not connected, you will see a message after you press the "Delete" button that asks you if you really want to delete this message. (This is a safeguard to give you a chance to reverse your decision.) Point the cursor on either the "Yes" or the "No" button and click. Another way to do this is to press the "Y" or "N" key on the keyboard. The message is now gone. (If you wish to delete a message that you have already opened, just follow the same procedure.)

Setting Up an ISP Account

If no one has helped you to set up an account, go to the left side of your desktop. There you will see several icons. Point the cursor on the one that looks like an "e" and says "Internet Explorer." Press the left mouse button twice (double-click). Follow the instructions for setting up an account. Or you can put the America Online CD into the CD drive and follow the installation instructions for a free trial period of 100 (or more) hours. This is plenty of time to learn how to do a variety of tasks. Then you can choose which ISP you would like to use.

Your E-Mail Address

Your e-mail address consists of two parts. The first is your user name, which you get to choose. The second part tells everyone which ISP you are using. YOU MUST GIVE PEOPLE YOUR *WHOLE* E-MAIL ADDRESS. It is like the street, city, state, and zip code that you use to receive regular mail (cutely referred to as "snail mail" by the computer crowd). To just say, "my address is JCL" or "my address is .com" is the equivalent of giving your home address as "Paul" or "803…." Your letters and magazines would never arrive at your house, and the same is true for e-mail.

Here's another important piece of advice about e-mail. If you have a friend or acquaintance with whom you rarely speak (you know the one—the person you don't want to have much to do with, but you were raised to be polite so you get together every few months for lunch), and he or she asks you if you have an e-mail address, your answer is *NO!* You *do not* have to be polite about *everything!* If you do not want to talk on the telephone with this person, why would you want to receive "mail" every day from him or her? If you really are that polite, you will feel the need to write back to them. Now you have a "relationship" with someone you don't even want to see regularly.

6

Chapter Six
More to the Internet than Just E-Mail:
The World Wide Web Is Waiting!

I told you there were other things to notice as you look at the America Online (AOL) "Welcome" window. The first important item is on the right of the window and says "My Weather." The current temperature for your area is shown just underneath the heading. Better yet, if you point the cursor on the words "My Weather" and press the left mouse button once (click), a new window appears with both current and future forecasts. This is even better than the Weather Channel!

In the same "Welcome" window you will see the name of the city or town where you live. (It is usually at the bottom of the window near the middle, or it is in a vertical list on the left side of the window. This has a list of all sorts of interesting things.) If you point the cursor on your city name and press the left mouse button once (click), a new window will appear with information telling you what is happening around your town. Aside from special events and news, you can usually get current movie listings. This is a lot easier than going to the newspaper!

Figure 6.1

Click on "Internet" to type in a Web site address and get on the World Wide Web.
Click on "Quotes" to get any stock quotations.

Press these arrows to go forward or back a page.

Click on "My Weather" for the latest forecast your area.

Click on "Set My Places" to personalize the window to your interests.

When you have some time, you might want to try pointing the cursor on any of the items on the left side of this window and clicking on the left mouse button. Take the time to look over the different bits of information in each area. It is good practice and you might find a favorite item or area. Remember, if you do not want to see a particular window, go to the backward arrow on the left side of the toolbar. For each left click you will go back one page.

Those Dedicated to Watching the Stock Market—This Is Your Section
(Non-Portfolio Watchers, Skip This Section and Go To "Surfing The Web")

Something else to notice on the AOL "Welcome" window is a heading on the lower right side called "My Places." Just under that heading is a box with the heading "Set My Places." If you point the cursor on this box and press the left mouse button (click), you are given a new window and offered five settings (see figure 6.2). Make the first one "My Portfolios." This is your entrance to the stock market! Just point the cursor on this title, click, and you are connected to the latest Wall Street information. You can even customize the screen by adding a folder of your own investments. Then, every time you click on "My Portfolios" and open to the name of a particular portfolio, a listing of all your positions will appear along with their current price and other information (see figure 6.3).

Figure 6.2

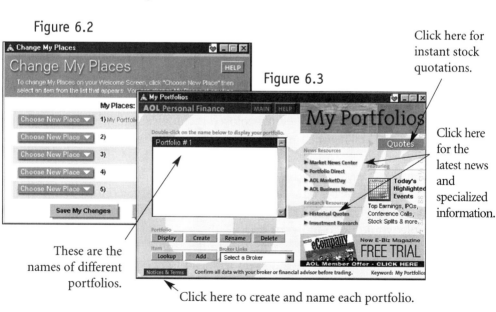

Figure 6.3

Click here for instant stock quotations.

Click here for the latest news and specialized information.

These are the names of different portfolios.

Click here to create and name each portfolio.

You might want to have your most recent brokerage statement next to you to make it easier to "fill in all the blanks." After pointing the cursor on "My Portfolios," press the left mouse button once (click). A new window will appear and you will see the words "My Portfolios" in black letters on a multicolored background. For instant stock quotations you can just point the cursor below this where it says "Quotes" and click. Then fill in the symbol (letters that identify each company) in the appropriate space. Another way you can get current stock quotations is by going directly to the icon bar and finding the second icon from the right, which shows a "$" over the word "Quotes." Point the cursor at this icon and press the left mouse button once (click) to get individual stock prices and information.

This new window has a large box within which you can place the names of all the different portfolios you wish to create. (Let me mention that you may also just want one of your children to put all your financial information on the computer for you. They may think that it is easier to use another program like Quicken® to manage and record your financial information. However, there is no reason that you cannot do this all yourself as it is really not that difficult—and after all, this is why you bought this guide. I personally think it is a lot of fun to "check in" once a day or so and see what is happening "on The Street.")

So assuming that you wish to continue, look in the lower left corner of the window. You will see four colored rectangles with white letters (see figure 6.3) The one on the left says "Create." Point the cursor on this box and press the left mouse button once (click). A new window will appear that says "Step 1: New Portfolio Setup" on the title bar. The cursor will be blinking in the box in which you need to type a name. All you have to do is think of a name you wish to use. An example would be to use your initials, the name of the brokerage house where this account is held, or simply "mine." Then follow the prompt on the lower right side that tells you to press "Next." The name you have given this portfolio will appear in the previous window's message box when you have finished setting things up! (see figure 6.3).

Now we get to the difficult part. Look at this next window ("Step 2"). This one requires a lot of information. That is why it would be helpful to have your most recent brokerage statement in front of you. (See figure 6.4.)

Figure 6.4

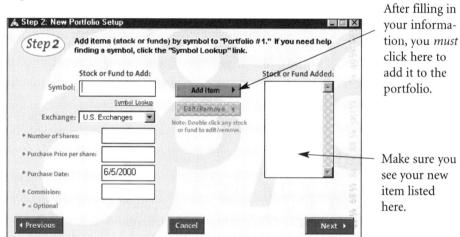

After filling in your information, you *must* click here to add it to the portfolio.

Make sure you see your new item listed here.

Go ahead and type in the necessary information in each of the appropriate boxes. Remember: The easiest way to move from box to box is to press the "Tab" key *lightly!* (The alternative is to place the cursor in each box and press the left mouse button once.) You may also add "cash" to your portfolio, but you need to do that as a separate addition as the computer will warn you! When you have put in as much information as you wish (you do not have to fill in every box), point the cursor on the "Add Item" button to the right and press the left mouse button once (click).

A dialog box will appear telling you that this particular position has been added to whatever your portfolio name is. Point the cursor on the "Next" button and press the left mouse button once to move to the next window ("Step 3"), which allows you to add cash and use indices. Congratulations! You have now started to create a working portfolio all by yourself! Now, click on the "Finish" button.

53

Finally in this window, click on your new portfolio—the name you gave it should be highlighted. It will open and the positions you just added are now displayed. (You can go back and add more positions by pointing the cursor on the "Add" button near the bottom and clicking.)

The information in front of you will tell you the symbol of your position, the current/closing price, the change, your gains/losses based on your purchase price information, and the current value of this position. Look at the bottom of the window, you have lots of other options to choose from, so just go ahead and click on whatever interests you. Have fun!

Surfing the Web

Now it is time to start "surfing the Web." This can be a lot of fun or totally frustrating. It is fun to see all the companies, organizations, and government agencies that can give you interesting information. You can learn about new products, get the exhibition schedule for your local museum, see what stories will be presented on the television show "60 Minutes," read a magazine or newspaper and get the local movie schedule, etc., etc. You can even connect with the Web page of foreign cities and plan details of a future trip. These are the fun parts.

The frustrating part is that sometimes you are given too much information. It is difficult to sort through everything to get to the special item that interests you. Sorry, that is just the way it is right now. Once you have found a particular "home page" that you like or need you can "mark" it by making it one of your "Favorites" so that you can get back to it quickly. However getting to that in the first place takes thought and patience.

AOL version 5.0 makes this a little easier for you, as it allows you to pick five areas called "My Places." Look at the lower right side of the AOL "Welcome" window (see figures 6.1 and 6.2). Under "My Places" is a box with "Set My Places." Point the cursor on this box and press the left mouse button once (click). You now have a great number of choices of areas that might interest you. Within each area there are subheadings to narrow down your choices. Follow the prompts to pick five areas that you want to "get to" quickly. These will then be available immediately every time you log on.

So back to actually searching for something in particular. The best is to just jump in and try it out. Notice that in the large AOL window there is a title bar (the blue line) at the top, a menu bar (a gray line with the title of each menu) just below, and then a line with multicolored rectangles. Under that line is another gray line. In the middle of this fourth line there is a box that says "Type Keyword or Web Address here and click GO." Point the cursor in this box, press the left mouse button *once* to *highlight* the current words in the box. Then type in a word—"the keyword"—that describes whatever it is that interests you. Or type in a Web address that you have gotten from an article, an advertisement, or from television. (You can tell it is a Web address as it will begin "www." followed by the name of the company, group or institution and then completed with the famous ".com" or ".org" etc.; see figure 6.5.)

Figure 6.5

You can easily get on the Internet: "Type Keyword or Web Address here and click GO."

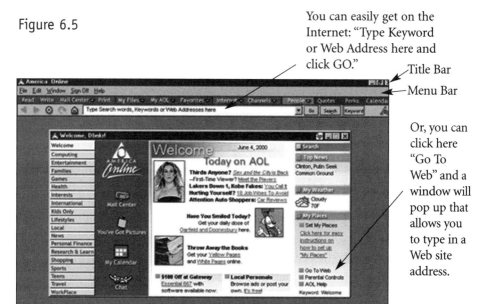

Title Bar

Menu Bar

Or, you can click here "Go To Web" and a window will pop up that allows you to type in a Web site address.

Now this is just practice. You do not need to agonize over what to type. Pick anything! If you want a suggestion, try typing in www.cbs.com and then press the "Enter" key. This will connect you to the Web page of this famous television company. Another idea is to type in the word "gastrointestinal." Wait until you see the possibilities of *that* keyword! (Note: The online bookseller barnesandnoble.com is ready to offer you lots of books on this subject if you click on their "link" on the left side of the window.) My mother wanted to look at the Web page for the Metropolitan Opera in New York City so she typed in www.metopera.org. Now she knows everything about the upcoming season. One of my favorites is www.bluemountain.com, a source of free electronic greeting cards. Not only do they have cards for *every* occasion, not only will they send as many "electronic" cards as you like to as many people as you like for free, but they also can send greeting cards in a dozen different languages!

After you have typed in something, wait a moment and you will see a page that offers you all sorts of information pertaining to the organization or group. You can place your cursor on whatever you like and press the left mouse button once (click). If you wait, another page will appear giving you the information you asked for and offering you "links" to additional information or offering other choices.

Please note the following:

• If something is written in blue and underlined, this is a "link" and pointing the cursor on it and pressing the left mouse button once will take you straight to that information.

• If you want to see the previous page, go to the "back" arrow at the extreme left of the lowest gray line.

• After you have gone back a page or two, you can go forward again by clicking on the "forward" arrow just to the right of the "back" arrow. (Think of the arrows as similar to those on the controls of your VCR—another piece of electronic equipment that might frustrate you!)

• Look at all the items at the top and bottom of most Web pages, as they really help guide you around the "site" and also help get you back to the beginning or "home page."

• You do not need to know the address of a Web site. You can experiment and see if you get what you want. How? Type in "www." followed by the name you think your group would use, followed by ".com" if it is commercial, ".edu" if it is an educational institution, or ".org" if it is a nonprofit. Then press "Enter." If it works, great! If not, try to think of another name that they would use and try again. This is also the time to try a "keyword." Fill in the word or words that describe what you want to know about or need. Then press the "Enter" key. Look over the list that is provided in your category and select whatever looks best. (You can always "go back" to the original list and try another choice.)

• Another way to try and find something is to use what is called a "search engine." Examples are www.yahoo.com, www.google.com, www.northernlight.com, www.alltheweb.com, and www.altavista,com. These are sites that are specifically designed to find information for you—information that is written in a more complete and easily understood format. With more than a billion Web sites, it is impossible for any of these "engines" to search all but a relatively small percentage of the Web. However, new search engines are appearing every week. It is well worth trying each of these to see which ones work best for you.

• When you get tired of all this just shut it down! How? By pointing the cursor on the "X" in the top right corner of the Web page and pressing the left mouse button once (clicking). Now you can play one of the nice card games or just go read a book!

• There is obviously more to learn about the "Web," but this is a start!

• For a number of Web site addresses that I think might be of interest to you, please check Appendix C.

7

Chapter Seven

Some Simple Basic Fun???
This Is Like the Piano!
Do I Really Have to
Practice One Hour a Day?

The *bad* news is that it would really be
helpful if you played with the computer
every day for about an hour. The *good*
news is that you do not have to do "work"!
One of your tasks is to play some of the
games that come with your computer.

If your nice young person followed the suggestions in Chapter 2, you should have an icon on the left side of your desktop that looks like a deck of cards and says "Solitaire." Let's start with that game.

You know the drill by now—point the cursor on the solitaire icon and press the left mouse button twice (double-click). The cards are waiting in front of you. If you do not know how to play the game, go to the "Help" menu. (Remember the easy way is to press the "Alt" key and the "H" key simultaneously, or you can put the cursor on Help and press the left mouse button once (click).) Help Topics will give you a number of hints about playing the game. Just move the arrow key down to highlight the topic you want to see and press the "Enter" key.

If you do know how to play the game, terrific. However, you are probably wondering how to move the cards! Do you remember that I told you that you would need to know how to "click and drag"? Well this is where you can practice!

Place the cursor on the card that you wish to move. *Hold down* the left mouse button. *While holding down the left mouse button,* move the mouse over to the card on which you wish to place your card. Then release the left mouse button.

If the card moved to the right spot, congratulations! You are a natural! However it is just as likely that the card popped back into its original column. What might have happened is that you released the left mouse button too soon. Do not worry. That is just fine. In fact that is great because this is the reason you are playing a card game. You do not have to tell anyone that you are playing solitaire. Instead tell them that you are practicing "clicking and dragging"!

Having said that, go ahead and try to move the card again. Keep doing this and as you get better you will see that you do not have to grip the mouse quite so hard. (In addition you will learn that you do not have to twist your hand/arm/shoulder to get the cursor to the right spot! Visualization and "body English" do not help in any sport—even computer games! Remember, when you are about to go off the mouse pad, lift up the mouse and place it back in the middle of the mouse pad.)

If you have no move, it is time to go to the deck of cards in the upper left corner of the game board. Place the cursor on the deck and press the left mouse button once (click). The third card is turned over. Do this again and the next "third" card is revealed. If you can use any of these cards, you need to place the cursor on the card, press the left mouse button and, *while holding down the left mouse button,* move the card where it should go. Then release the left mouse button.

When you have come to the last card, you will see a large circle to show you that you have run through the whole deck. If you want to go through the deck again, just point the cursor on the circle and press the left mouse button once (click). The whole thing starts over again. You can change some of the rules of the game by pointing the cursor on the "Game" menu and pressing the left mouse button once (clicking) to bring down the menu. Point the cursor on "Options," press the left mouse button once, then make the choices you want. Be sure to point the cursor on "OK" and click so the computer makes the changes.

When you have given up on the game you have been dealt, or when you are ready to play a new hand, go to the "Game" menu and click on "Deal." (Remember the other way to do this is Alt+G and then D). Now you are ready to start over.

Figure 7.1

The menu bar with two choices, Game or Help

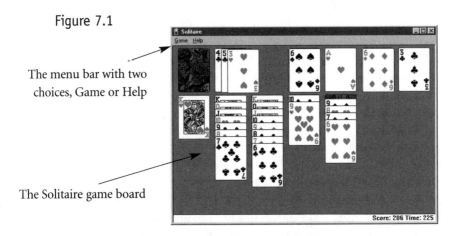

The Solitaire game board

There are several other card games that you might like to try. Notice that each one has a different technique for moving the cards. Either read the directions or just go ahead and try different things. You might find it unsettling to have the format and computer instructions change from one game to the next. Please understand that each game or program is created by a different group of people. They do things the way that they think works best. This is just something you have to live with. What is intuitive for them will probably be foreign to you in the beginning. Keep at it. I promise it will soon be comfortable.

A personal note: From experience I can tell you that the computer does not deal easy games. I have spent most of the night trying to "beat" the machine. I was visiting my mother to help her with her new computer, but she could not practice her new skills because I was determined to continue playing solitaire until I won!

Chapter Eight

Writing Documents and Correspondence:
I Am Already in the Middle of the Book and I Still Don't Know How to Write a Letter!

I am sympathetic with your frustration, but if this is the most important task on your list, I am sure that you have skipped ahead to this chapter!

Explaining how to produce and save documents and correspondence is probably the most difficult section of this book. It is difficult, since there are several programs that you can use to do the same tasks. It is difficult since each program works in a slightly different way. It is difficult since each of these writing programs offers more choices, more icons, more menu bars, and more ways for things to go wrong than any other program you will use. Finally it is the most difficult as many of us are still trying to learn what half of these things do ourselves!

Once again, rather than discussing all the different programs available, I will explain how to do some basic tasks using a program with which I am familiar and which I feel is very "user-friendly." That program is Microsoft Word. This is not to say that one program is better than another. In fact I think Corel's WordPerfect® is also an easy program to use. It is just that I would like this book and these instructions to be slightly shorter than the Manhattan telephone directory!

Whichever program you choose to use as your primary document writing program, the most important thing to remember is to *save all your work*, and do it as you are going along. *Everyone* is told this and *no one* bothers to do it. That is, they do not bother to "save as they go along" until a very important paper or letter is suddenly lost after they have spent half a day working on it! One experience like this and one learns to "save" every 5 to 10 minutes. (While writing this book, I was pressing the "Ctrl" key and the "S" key to save things after almost every paragraph. Whenever I stopped to think about the next phrase, or whenever I made a correction, it was my natural reflex!) There's more on "saving your work" later in this chapter, but let me mention that much depends on which word-processing program you are using. The program WordPerfect saves automatically. Microsoft Word does not, but it can be set up so that it does. This is another thing that your helper can adjust for you at the start.

Now Can I Write a Letter to My Cousin in England?

Assuming that Microsoft Word® is a program on your computer, we are now ready to start. You will first need to make this program the "active" window on your desktop. If your helpful young person has done as asked, you should have an icon on the left side of the desktop that has a large blue "W" and says "Microsoft Word." If this is so, point the cursor on this icon and press the left mouse button twice (double-click).

If the icon is *not* on the desktop, do the following:
1. Press the Windows key. It is the one that looks like a flag on the keyboard—lowest row, on the left.
2. Use the up arrow key to highlight "Programs."
3. Use the right arrow key to show all the programs.
4. Move the arrow key to highlight the program that is called Microsoft Word.
5. Press the "Enter" key.

Figure 8.1

The "Start" menu with expanded menus

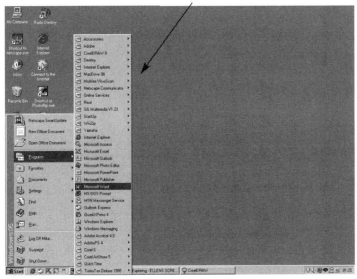

Now you should be looking at a large window with the words "Microsoft Word – Document1" on the title bar (see figure 8.2). The cursor will be blinking in the large open area that looks like a piece of paper. You are now ready to write anything you want! Just start typing!

So if it was this easy, why didn't I tell you all this sooner? Well the reason for waiting is that if you look just below the title bar you will see three rows of words and icons. At this point in the book, you are probably starting to feel comfortable with a menu bar. All that has been added to this one are some tools that you may or may not want to use when you write. The other bars are also types of "toolbars." One is the "standard" toolbar and the other is the "format" toolbar. (Some versions of this program may have both of these toolbars on one line—this is not a problem.)

Another thing to understand is that most of the icons you see on these two toolbars are also items that you will find if you press the left mouse button on any of the words on the menu bar. These are just quicker ways to do certain things. (They are quicker if you like using the mouse. Otherwise you will find it helpful to have the menu bar in order to use keystrokes to give different commands.)

Figure 8.2

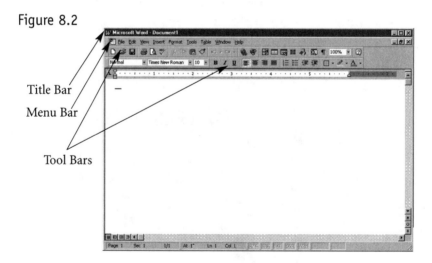

Title Bar

Menu Bar

Tool Bars

Figure 8.3

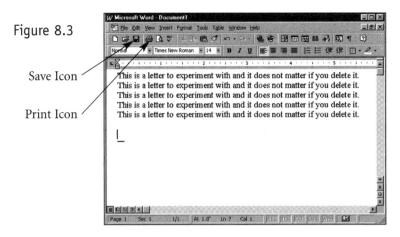

Save Icon

Print Icon

If you have something specific that you want to write right away, please go ahead and start typing. When you are done with the letter or list, point the cursor on the icon that looks like a printer on the toolbar (the third line, fourth item) and press the left mouse button twice (double-click). Then skip ahead to page 77 to the section on saving your work. You can come back to this next part whenever you want to learn how to do more with this program.

For those who are not in a hurry, it is time to experiment. As this is not an important letter or your holiday shopping list, it does not matter if you wipe out whole paragraphs or recopy the same line five times. This is just a fun way to learn.

Let's start at the beginning. In front of you is something that looks like a white piece of paper. The first thing we will do is pretend to write a letter to Cousin Doris in London. Go ahead and write a letter the way you would on any typewriter. If you like you can copy my letter so that we can work on the formatting together step by step. Here is my letter:

The First Week with My New PC

Dear Doris,

I am happy to hear that all is well and that you had a lovely holiday in the country. I can imagine that the garden must look wonderful after all the rain you had last month. I hope that your visitors from Switzerland appreciated all the work and preparation that went into this.

Everything is fine here. I have been totally occupied—day and night—with my newest "toy." I bought myself a COMPUTER! I know you will think I am crazy, but I really wanted to communicate with Beth and Paul on a regular basis, and they tell me that the best way to do this is to "e-mail" them. I also want to be able to make corrections easily when typing a letter rather than redoing everything several times because I forgot a line. In addition, you would not believe the fun I am having looking up things on the "World Wide Web"!

Then my friend Silvia told me about some wonderful games that I can play on the computer. I am sometimes up late at night unable to stop until I "beat" the computer. I know it sounds silly, but my orthopedic surgeon told me the computer is as good as knitting for arthritis prevention, and I really think that the games are helping me keep my fingers and hands more flexible.

Well that is all for now. Let me know what you think of all this. More importantly, if you have an e-mail address, please send it to me. Think of all the money we will save on postage and telephone calls if we use the Internet!

Love,

Now if you are like me, you made lots of little typing errors while writing your letter or copying mine. (Again, if you just copy my letter, it might make it easier to follow some of the things I tell you to do.)

Spell Check—Your Own Personal Editor

The first thing I would like to mention is that as you were typing you may have noticed that some of your words were underlined in red or green. If you stopped to look at the words underlined in red, you may have noticed that they were spelled incorrectly. Perhaps you "backspaced" when you saw an error and retyped the word. Another way of making a correction is to point the cursor to the right of the wrong letter(s) and press the left mouse button (click). You are placing the cursor at a certain spot, the insertion point, so that you can make a change. Now you can use the "Backspace" key to erase the mistake and then retype the correct letters. (After you are done with your corrections, be sure to point the cursor and click at the spot where you wish to continue typing. This is the insertion point. Otherwise you may find your next paragraph in the middle of your first sentence. It is something we all do in the beginning because we forget!)

Now if you did not notice this happening or you do not see any red lines, you are either an excellent speller and typist, or you should go back and look at the letter to see if there really is some red underlining that you have missed! Red underlining means a misspelled word and green underlining means the computer did not like the grammar you used. One of the nice features of this program is that you can rush ahead typing all your thoughts and not worry about some misspelled words; when you are done you can use "Spell Check" to make the necessary corrections. It also helps those who do not spell very well, as it points out words that might have been assumed to be correct. (Note: If you don't see any red lines and you know that you have some typing errors, it is possible that your Spell Check feature is not activated; have you helper turn it on for you.)

To have the computer check your work, point the cursor at the icon that has the letters "ABC" over a blue check mark. (It's on the toolbar, third line down, sixth icon from the left.) Press the left mouse button once (click) and a window will appear with your misspelled word or grammatically incorrect phrase in the top half of the box. Suggestions for changes are in the box below. To the right you are given choices which include making or ignoring the suggested change, or canceling the Spell Check (see figure 8.4).

Figure 8.4

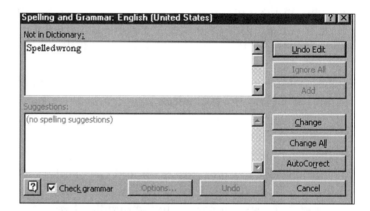

Figure 8.5

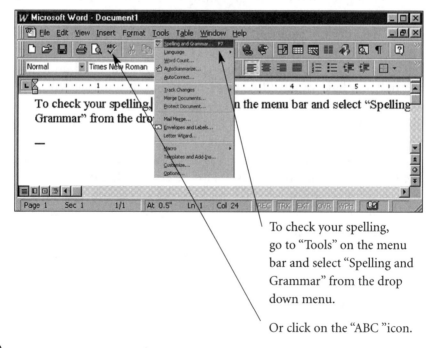

To check your spelling, go to "Tools" on the menu bar and select "Spelling and Grammar" from the drop down menu.

Or click on the "ABC" icon.

By pointing the cursor on your choice and pressing the left mouse button once, the computer will do whatever it is that you want to do. You can also get to Spell Check from the menu bar. Press the "Alt" key and the "T" key at the same time (Alt+T). The "Tools" menu will appear. The top choice is "Spelling and Grammar." Press the "S" key and you have opened "Spell Check." (See figures 8.6 and 8.7.)

Figures 8.6 and 8.7

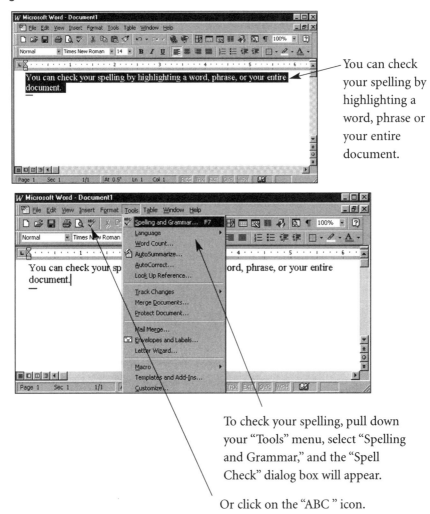

You can check your spelling by highlighting a word, phrase or your entire document.

To check your spelling, pull down your "Tools" menu, select "Spelling and Grammar," and the "Spell Check" dialog box will appear.

Or click on the "ABC " icon.

You can also check individual words as you go along by highlighting the underlined word and then starting Spell Check in one of the two ways described above. After checking the highlighted word, Spell Check will ask if you want it to check the remainder of your document. You can either use the mouse to click on "Yes" or "No," or you can simply press the "Y" key for yes or the "N" key for no.

Formatting Your Work

Now, have you learned all the ways to highlight a word, phrase, or whole document? This is a very important skill. In Chapter 3 I explain how to do this using the "Shift" key and arrow keys. Reminder: Point the cursor at the beginning of the area to be highlighted and press the left mouse button (click). Hold down the "Shift" key. Move the arrow keys until everything you want is highlighted. Release the "Shift" key. Another way to do this is to place the cursor at the beginning or the end of the item you wish to highlight. Hold down the left mouse button and drag the mouse until everything you want is highlighted. Then release the left mouse button. Now you know why you had to practice "clicking and dragging" with the card games!

If you want to highlight your whole document it is even easier. Press the "Ctrl" key and the "A" key (Ctrl+A) at the same time and then release them. Notice that your whole document is now highlighted! Now you are probably wondering, "Why would I ever want to do that?"

When an item is highlighted it means you have told the computer that this is something with which you want to work. What does that mean? Maybe you want to take out a sentence or copy a phrase and move it somewhere else. Maybe you want to change the typeface or "font" or make something bigger or smaller. Maybe you want to make that phrase **bold**, or *italicized*, or underlined. You may choose to justify (line up) something to the left or to the right or to center it. When you highlight something, these are just some of the things you can do!

Look at the toolbar and the format bar. Point the mouse at each one of the icons and see what it says. Some of the pictures like the clean piece of paper or the printer really relate to what the icons do. Others might not be so obvious. That is why it is time to experiment.

Figure 8.8

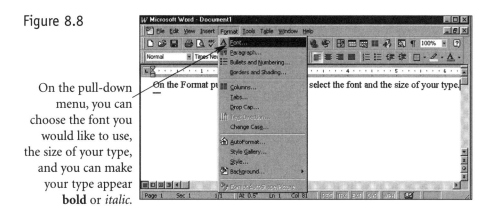

On the pull-down menu, you can choose the font you would like to use, the size of your type, and you can make your type appear **bold** or *italic*.

Figure 8.9

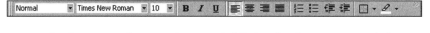

Go to the letter you have written. Highlight the first paragraph by pointing the cursor at the beginning of the first paragraph and pressing the left mouse button (click). Now hold down the "Shift" key and move the arrow keys down and right until the whole paragraph is highlighted. Now release the "Shift" key. (While this is the easiest, there are other ways to do this, including pointing the cursor at the start of the paragraph and then hold down the left mouse button. Drag the mouse to the right and down so that the whole paragraph is highlighted. Still another way to do this is to point the cursor in front of the first word in the first paragraph and click. Hold down the "Shift" key. Point the cursor at the end of the last word in the paragraph and press the left mouse button once (click). Release the "Shift" key.)

In *my* letter everything is highlighted from "I" to "this." Now point the cursor on the "**B**" (it even looks bold) on the format bar (the

73

lowest line) and press the left mouse button (click). Next "un-high-light" everything by moving the cursor anywhere on your "piece of paper" where nothing is written, and pressing once on the left mouse button. Look what happened! The whole paragraph is now in **bold** face.

Go to the next paragraph and highlight the first four words. (In my letter that is the sentence "Everything is fine here.") When it is high-lighted point the cursor on the "**I**" (notice it looks italicized), and press once on the left mouse button. "Un-highlight" everything by moving the cursor to an open part of your "piece of paper" and pressing the left mouse button. Now those first four words are *itali-cized*! Once again go ahead and highlight the next sentence. This time point the mouse button on the "U," which stands for underline, and press the left mouse button. Then un-highlight the sentence as you did before. Your next sentence is completely <u>underlined</u>!

Highlight your third paragraph. (You should really know how to do this now.) Look at the format bar (lowest line on the left side). There are several white boxes with black letters and numbers. Look at the one in the middle. It is telling you what font or typeface you are using right now. To change the font, point the cursor on the little down arrow to the right of the font name and press the left mouse button once (click). (See figure 8.9.)

A menu of different fonts will appear. You can now use the mouse or the down arrow key to scroll down the list of possibilities. (I know you do not know what most of these fonts look like. Right now that is not important as we are just playing. With practice you will find and, more importantly, remember which ones you really like. Then you can use them to make your notes more interesting.) Find the font called "Bookman Old Style" and when it is highlighted press the left mouse button. "Un-highlight" the third paragraph and look at the new font!

Highlight this paragraph again. Why not change the size of the font? To do this go to the box to the right, which has numbers. Point the cursor at the down arrow on the right. Press once on the left mouse button and then scroll down until another size, like "16," is highlighted. Press the left mouse button and then "un-highlight" the third paragraph.

The last thing I would like you to try is "cutting and pasting." Look at the last paragraph. In my letter the first sentence is, "Well that is all for now." Highlight that sentence and point the cursor on the icon that looks like a pair of scissors (toolbar, third row, seventh from the left). Press the left mouse button. The sentence is gone!

It is not really gone. It exists on a "clipboard" inside the computer. Point the cursor to the right of the last word in the last paragraph. **Important:** Press the left mouse button so that the cursor is blinking in that spot. Point the cursor at the icon to the right of the scissors on the toolbar—the one that looks like a clipboard (the icon is ninth from the left). Press the left mouse button once. The line you removed from the front of the paragraph is now at the end of the paragraph!

Point the cursor on the icon that looks like your printer (toolbar, third row, fourth from the left). Press the left mouse button once. Your letter is now being printed, assuming that you have turned on your printer. (The printer, like the computer, can be left on all the time. It makes things much easier and leaving it this way will not hurt it.)

Congratulations! You have just completed *nine* different tasks or changes to your letter, including printing it! You have really learned a great deal. Of course you can see that there are more icons and menus. However, this is a good beginning. You can always type up some other note and play with those words to see what the "other buttons" do!

By the way, if you would like to see what my letter looks like after all the changes, here it is (and I did a "copy" and "paste" to move it here!).

Dear Doris,

I am happy to hear that all is well and that you had a lovely holiday in the country. I can imagine that the garden must look wonderful after all the rain you had last month. I hope that your visitors from Switzerland appreciated all the work and preparation that went into this.

Everything is fine here. <u>I have been totally occupied–day and night–with my newest "toy."</u> I bought myself a COMPUTER! I know you will think I am crazy, but I really wanted to communicate with Beth and Paul on a regular basis, and they tell me that the best way to do this is to "e-mail" them. I also want to be able to make corrections easily when typing a letter rather than redoing everything several times because I forgot a line. In addition, you would not believe the fun I am having looking up things on the "World Wide Web"!

Then my friend Silvia told me about some wonderful games that I can play on the computer. I am sometimes up late at night unable to stop until I "beat" the computer. I know it sounds silly, but my orthopedic surgeon told me the computer is as good as knitting for arthritis prevention, and I really think that the games are helping me keep my fingers and hands more flexible.

Let me know what you think of all this. More importantly, if you have an "e-mail" address, please send it to me. Think of all the money we will save on postage and telephone calls if we use the Internet! Well that is all for now.

Love,

The Most Important Section in This Book:
SAVE SAVE SAVE

In order to begin to save something, it is easiest to have a new "piece of paper" or your "letterhead" open and ready to use in front of you. If you have the program Microsoft Word, all you have to do is point the cursor on the program icon, which should be sitting on your desktop or taskbar. Then press the left mouse button twice (double-click) and a window will open that is nothing more than "a blank piece of paper."

Notice that at the top of the window you have the title bar which at the moment says "Microsoft Word–Document1." Below that is the menu bar, a gray horizontal line, and below that is the toolbar with icons. The line below that is the format bar, it gives you a variety of options and controls for use in the document itself (everything from the size and typeface you wish to use, whether it is justified left or right, bold, underlined, in color, etc. etc.). Below that you have the "ruler," which helps you line up things on the page including indentations, etc.

On the menu bar go to the "File" menu by either pointing the cursor on the word "File" and pressing the left mouse button once (clicking), or by pressing the "Alt" key and the "F" key at the same time (Alt+F). A menu will drop down. Find the item that says "Save As." Highlight and open this by either moving the arrow key down to it and pressing the "Enter" key or by pointing the cursor on the item and pressing the left mouse button. (See figure 8.10.)

Figure 8.10

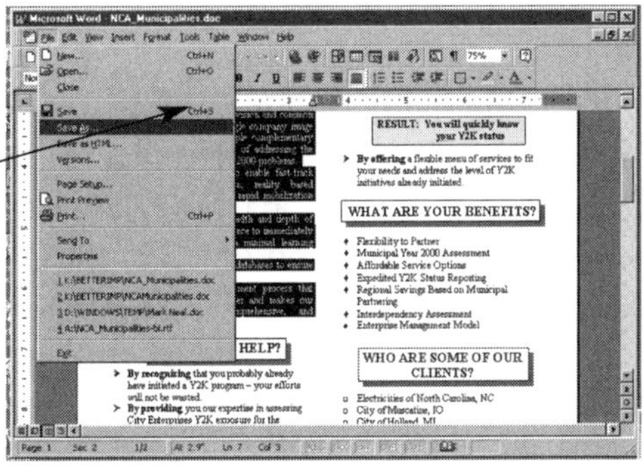

On the pull-down menu, you can start saving a document by clicking on "Save As."

A new window will open with "Save As" on the title bar followed by several white rectangles asking you where you want to save your document and what name you want to give it. This is a dialog box (see figure 8.11). There are also a number of icons, and on the right side you have the commands to "Save," "Cancel," "Options," "Save Versions." **The only ones you will need for now are the first two—save and cancel.**

Figure 8.11

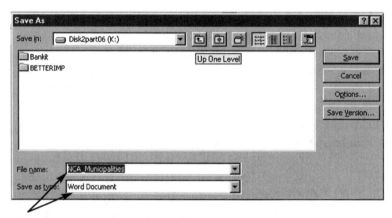

When you save your work, the file name you choose will appear in the top window, and how you have saved your document (such as "Word Document") will appear in the lower window.

Notice that near the bottom, the highlighted rectangle says "File Name." As it is highlighted, you can start typing the name of your document in this space without first placing the cursor in the box. (The name currently in that space is taken from the computer's memory of the first words you typed in this document. If you want, you can use this as your file name. However, it is better to pick something that will be really *meaningful* when you want to find the document in the future!)

After you give your document a name, you will need to decide into what folder you want it to go. Let's say you are keeping a folder devoted to your grandchild, Beth. This letter is a thank you note for all the help she gave you in setting up the computer. Therefore, you will want to place it in a folder named "Beth." (With this as an example, you might want to name your file "Beth-computer help-thanks.")

Your folder with the name "Beth" should be sitting in the larger folder called "My Documents." (Hopefully, all this was set up by your helpful young person or the computer expert you hired after reading Chapter 1! If not, look in Chapter 11.)

How do you get to the folder in which you want to save something? If for some reason the "Save in" box has the title of the correct folder, congratulations—you really are lucky! Most of the time you will need to find the correct folder.

Look in the large rectangular box below the "Save in" box. Is the name of the folder you want to use in there? If it is, then point the cursor at the correct folder and press the left mouse button twice (double-click). This folder will now appear in the "Save in" box. If you gave your file a name (as I told you to do first thing!), you can now point the cursor on "Save" and press the left mouse button (click). The dialog box will disappear and you may start typing your letter. (Note that in this example, your title bar will now read "Microsoft Word–Beth-computer help-thanks.doc" as this is the program and title of your document.)

If you do not see the folder you wish to use, it might be just one level up from the group of folders you are currently seeing. To move up one level, point the cursor on the yellow folder immediately to the right of the "Save in" box. It has an upward arrow in it and will also say "up one level" when the cursor rests on the icon. Press the left mouse button once and a new group of folders will appear. If the folder you wish to use is there, point the cursor on the desired folder and press the left mouse button twice (double-click). (See figure 8.12.)

Figure 8.12

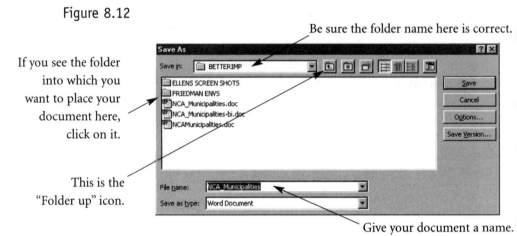

Be sure the folder name here is correct.

If you see the folder into which you want to place your document here, click on it.

This is the "Folder up" icon.

Give your document a name.

If you still can't find the right folder, try going up one more level. By now you will have found the correct folder for whatever it is that you are working on. The point is that it is important to try to save your work in the proper place so that you can find it again—and find it quickly! The computer is your file cabinet and you do not want to just throw all the papers into one big drawer! (Remember how you hate looking for your tax receipts, your birth certificate, your glasses, and the car keys.)

When everything is filled in correctly, place the cursor on "Save," press the left mouse button once, and you will have successfully saved your document. When you are ready to close your document and you have pressed the left mouse button on the "X" in the upper right corner, a dialog box will appear that will ask you if you want to save the changes you have made to this document. Please, just point the cursor on the "Yes" button and press the left mouse button once (click). It cannot hurt to save everything. You can think about it later and delete it if necessary!

Chapter Nine

Other Ways to Get Information and Have Fun, or, What Do I Do with All These CDs and Did I Have to Pay Extra for All This Stuff?

Your computer comes with a number of programs and compact disks that you will probably never use. They are "bundled" together and so in a sense you did not pay extra for these things. But at the same time, the computer company will not give you a rebate if you do not want them!

One of the great items that *may* come with the computer is a software program that is an encyclopedia (usually Encarta). If not, it is something worth purchasing. Something that I still do not understand is how all the information on a whole bookshelf can be "put on" something the size of one or two compact disks. But it does not matter how they do it—the fact is that all *you* have to do is put the Encarta Encyclopedia CD into your CD drive and watch what happens!

Within a moment, the screen will fill with a lovely picture while words scroll in front of you and music plays! This is the program opening up and getting ready for your use. You then have a number of options. As with most programs, you can first get an "overview" or "tutorial" of all that Encarta can do. Just point the cursor on the word "Overview" and press the left mouse button twice (double-click). Also note that there is an underlined letter in most of the word options. If you press the "Alt" key and the underlined letter key, it will open that area.

While it is always good to follow any tutorial you are offered, I also understand that you just want to "look something up"! With that in mind point the cursor at the top where it says something about "find" and press the left mouse button once (click). You can then just type in the word or name of whatever you want. On the left side of the window you will soon see a list of a number of articles on your subject. Point the cursor on the desired article and press the left mouse button twice (double-click) and it will then appear. Just use your arrow keys to move down the page in order to read the whole article.

Alternatively, you can place the cursor on the scroll bar on the right side of the window and hold down the left mouse button to scroll down and see more of the article. (You may have noticed that sometimes only the left or right part of a document or page is visible. If you look at the bottom of the window you will see something that looks like the scroll bar, but is horizontal. By pointing the cursor on the arrows to the right and left and holding down the left mouse button, you can move the page over to make more of it visible. See figure 9.1.)

Figure 9.1

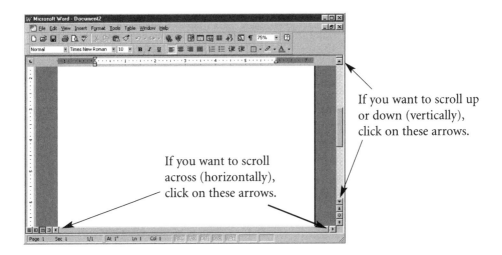

If you want to scroll up or down (vertically), click on these arrows.

If you want to scroll across (horizontally), click on these arrows.

Now keep going, there is more for you to find! For every article there are related subjects. If you are interested in learning more about a subject, you might want to go to one of these "links." Most of the time it is easy to tell if something is a "link." It will be written in blue and underlined. Point the cursor on the blue, underlined word and press the left mouse button once (click). Did you notice that the cursor looked like a hand with a pointing finger when it touched the link? (Reminder: The cursor will take on different "looks" depending on the task that it is doing.)

Another way to find more information is to look in the upper right section of the window. There you will find the "Information" symbol and words to help you continue with your search. (The left side also has a menu bar. Use it the same way you use all the other menu bars.) If you want the most recent information about your subject you can even go "on-line" to the Internet *automatically*. Follow the prompts that you are given by the computer when it asks if you want to connect to the Internet.

The very best thing about all this is that you can just *play* with it! You cannot lose information or wipe out anything that is on your CD. You can open as many windows or ask to find as many things as you want. It is another great way of getting to know how to make your computer work for you.

Finally, just remember that if you want to get rid of a window because you feel "overloaded," go to the upper right corner of the window and point your cursor on the "X." Then press the left mouse button once (click). If you are really frustrated and just want to have everything stop, go to the keyboard and press the "Ctrl" key and the "F4" key (Ctrl + F4) simultaneously. This will close any window.

While we are discussing loading and unloading CDs, I should mention that you can use your computer and the CD drive to listen to audio compact disks while you work. If you place an audio CD into the CD drive it should start playing right away. Obviously there is only one CD drive so you cannot listen to music while you are using other disks like the encyclopedia or Scrabble. However, for most other things it is nice to have the entertainment. Go to Chapter 11 for complete details on how to play an audio CD and control the volume.

You are now asking yourself, "How do I put the compact disk into the CD drive?" On the tower of the computer (the box that is the "brains" of the machine) there are several slots. One of these is for CDs and another is for "floppy" disks. Hopefully, your helpful young person has shown you where these are and how to put things in and take things out of them. Some computers even have the slots labeled. Notice that there is a button that you can press to open the CD drive and when you press the button a "holder" for the CD slides out. Place the CD in the holder—the side with words goes up—and press the button again to have the holder retract into the tower. Everything should just start working on its own. (If not, see Appendix A, Trouble Shooting.) To take the CD out, just press the button again, take out your CD, and close the drive by pressing the button one more time.

10
Chapter Ten
The Start Menu and All the Other Things That Have Not Yet Been Discussed

Here we are near the end of the book and you are probably wondering why I have not mentioned something as basic as the "Start" menu. Well there are a whole lot of reasons, including the fact that this is my book and this is the order that I thought was most useful! In addition I would imagine that you have looked in the Index or Chapter 11, and you have seen that there is a section devoted to the "Start" menu.

Basically the "Start" menu is the way to "get to" *everything* in your computer. It is your access to programs and settings. It also has the "Help" folder and a way of "finding" anything you have lost. The most recent documents that you have worked on are all seen when you highlight "Documents." (If you highlight one of the documents by using your arrow keys, you can then open it by pressing the "Enter" key. Immediately you can pick up exactly where you left off. See figure 10.1.)

Figure 10.1

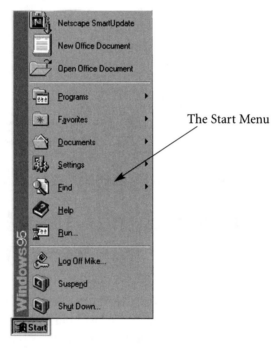

The Start Menu

However, what is most important is that with the "Start" menu you can restart or turn off the computer *properly*. When you are ready to turn off the computer, it is best to close all the windows on the desktop. You do this by pointing the cursor on the "X" on the extreme right of each title bar. Then press the left mouse button once (click). Another way to do this is to press the "Alt" key and the "F" key (Alt+F) at the same time. The "File" menu will drop down. Notice that the word "Exit" has the "x" underlined. This shows you that if you press the "X" key on the keyboard you will exit or close this program.

To use the "Start" menu first press the Windows key (it resembles a flag and is on the bottom row of the keyboard on the left side). The "Start" menu will appear and just above the word "Start" are the words "Shut Down." Press the up arrow key once and this will be highlighted. Now press the "Enter" key and a new window will appear. This is a dialog box. Note that the rest of the desktop is shaded to emphasize that you are about to do something important! (See figures 10.2 and 10.3.)

Figure 10.2

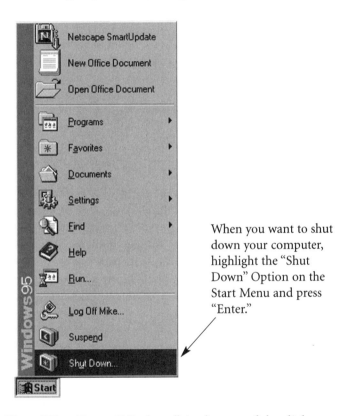

When you want to shut down your computer, highlight the "Shut Down" Option on the Start Menu and press "Enter."

The title bar will say "Shut Down Windows." At the top of the dialog box will be the question, "What do you want the computer to do?" You have several choices, but the only ones to consider right now are either "Shut down" or "Restart." If things do not seem to be working properly or you have added a new program then you may want to "Restart" your computer. However, there is nothing wrong with shutting everything down totally. (In fact if your modem has "taken over" your telephone line, as mine sometimes does, the only way to clear it is to shut off the computer completely. Don't worry, I seem to be the only one in my family who has this problem!)

Once you have made a choice, you can press the "Enter" key and the computer will do the rest! If you realize that you do not want to do this at all, just press "Cancel." The third alternative is to press "Help" and check other possibilities. (See figure 10.3.)

Figure 10.3

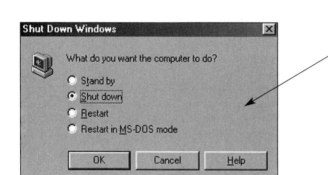

The "Shut Down" Window gives you options: You can click on OK to shut down the computer; you can restart; you can get help—or you can cancel the command.

Another reason for mentioning the "Start" menu is that this is your access to the control panel. This is one of the most important features on the computer and also a lot of fun with which to play. Press the Windows key (the one that looks like a flag) and then use the up arrow to highlight the sixth item from the bottom. It is called "Settings." Use the right arrow key to show all the items under "Settings." The one at the top and the one that will be highlighted is "Control Panel." Press the "Enter" key and a new window will appear that is filled with 20 to 25 icons! DO NOT PANIC! You *do not* have to do anything with all of this. (See figures 10.4 and 10.5.)

Figure 10.4

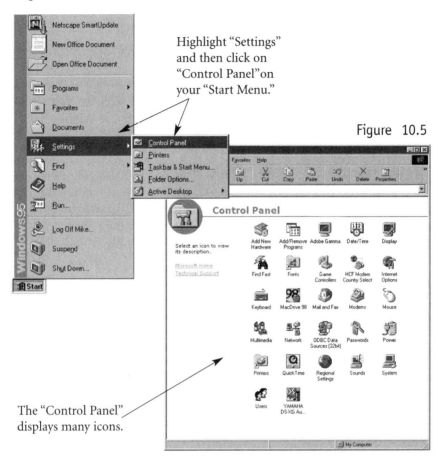

Highlight "Settings"
and then click on
"Control Panel"on
your "Start Menu."

Figure 10.5

The "Control Panel"
displays many icons.

However, if you are interested in changing the way your mouse moves
around the desktop, or the size and style of your fonts (typefaces), or if
you want everything you write to be printed in green, this is the place
to make those changes. By placing the cursor on one of these icons and
pressing the left mouse button twice (double-clicking), a number of
dialog boxes become available. Each one offers you choices with
changes you can make. You can always go back to the "default" or
original settings. This just gives you a chance to make things more
individual or easier to use.

As for all the other things that have not been discussed, I have several thoughts about this. There are many different computer books on the market. It is my feeling that if you feel comfortable with all the items covered in this book, you are ready to try one of those "big, thick books." You might find them a bit intimidating after reading this book. However, all you need to do is look in the index for a keyword that covers your question. Then just read those few paragraphs or that section. If you have gone all through this book, you have the skills and the vocabulary to understand most things that the "big boys" throw at you!

My other thought is that this is a basic, introductory book on computers. Nonetheless, it has given you a lot of information. If you choose only to work and play with the items I have covered, you will be doing an awful lot. In some cases, you will be using your computer more than the majority of people I know! (Maybe some of my friends should buy this book so they can get more use out of their expensive machines.)

Whatever you decide, never let a book or a person intimidate you. It is your computer and you can use it any way you want!

11

Chapter Eleven
A *Step-By-Step* Guide for Each Task

How to Connect All the New Equipment

The different components of your system will all plug into the back
of your PC. (This is the "tower"—the brains of your system.) Refer to
the diagram that came with your assembly instructions as you follow
the directions below.

1. Do not plug anything into an electrical outlet at this time!

2. Take the cord from the keyboard and plug it into the tower. It
   is a round plug that goes into a round port on the tower.
   (Check the diagram sent with the computer as well as the
   instructions.)

3. Take the cord from the mouse (the oval item that is the size of
   the palm of your hand with a ball on its underside) and plug it
   into the other round port. (Check the diagram sent with the
   computer.)

4. There are two cords with plugs coming out of the monitor
   (the thing that looks like a TV). One is the power cord, so that
   plug is familiar. The other cord has a connector that has a
   funny shape and nine pins (male connection). Look at this
   plug and note that there are two rows, one with four and the
   other with five pins. Line up this "male" plug with the "female"
   serial port with nine holes on the back of the tower. Do not
   force anything—that means do not press too hard. With mod-
   erate pressure you can push this plug into the port.

5. The printer has a cable with a "male" and "female" connector.
   Usually the connector has 25 pins. Plug the "male" connector
   into the back of your tower. The parallel port on the PC has 25
   holes and sometimes has the symbol of a printer. Plug the
   "female" end of the cable into the printer itself.

6. If your modem is internal (it came with the computer and is
   inside the tower), you need to connect one end of the telephone cord to the back of the tower and the other end to a

telephone jack. If one is not close by, get a telephone extension cord. (See the list of "things to do while you wait" in Chapter 1!)

7. If your modem is external (not built-in) it will have a cord that plugs into the phone jack and the other end will plug into one of the serial ports on the back of the tower. (Serial ports are "male"connections with 9 or 25 pins sticking out. They are used to connect "peripherals," such as the printer, to the computer.) Look at and follow the instructions that come with the modem.

8. Now it is time to plug everything (PC, monitor, and printer) into an electrical outlet. You must plug these power cords into three-pronged (grounded) outlets. It is best to plug them into a "surge protector" and then plug the surge protector into the grounded outlet. A surge protector usually looks like an extension cord with a rectangular strip of outlets, a rocker switch, and a light to show that there is power. This will protect your expensive equipment from electrical mishaps. Just ask the person at the hardware store or the computer store to help you find one that meets your needs.

How to Add the Printer:

If your printer came with a CD then place the disk in the CD drive and wait for it to "turn on." A window will appear in front of you. Just point the cursor at the appropriate answer "button" (usually "Yes" or "Next") and press the left mouse button once (click) to answer each question as it appears. If there is no CD with your printer:

1. Press Windows key (on keyboard, looks like a flag, lowest row).

2. Use up arrow key to move up to "Settings." Items like "Settings" or "Programs" will have this symbol "▸"; this means there are more choices.

3. Press the right arrow key to see these choices or menu.

4. Press the down arrow key to highlight "Printers."

5. Press the "Enter" key to select "Printers."

6. Point the cursor at the icon "Add Printer" and press the left mouse button twice (double-click).

7. A window will appear called "Add Printer Wizard." Point the cursor at the word "Next" at the bottom of the window and press the left mouse button once (click on the "Next" button).

8. Use the arrow keys to highlight the name of the manufacturer and the model of your printer or point the cursor at the correct choices and press the left mouse button once to highlight it.

9. Point the cursor at the word "Next" at the bottom of the window and click.

10. Read each question that is asked and respond by pressing the "Y" for yes or the "N" for no. Then point the cursor at the word "Next" at the bottom of the window and press the left mouse button once (click on the "Next" button).

11. When you come to the last window, point the cursor at the word "Finish" and press the left mouse button (click on the "Finish" button). The printer is now installed.

Turning the Computer On—
Turning the Computer Off

To Turn On the Computer

1. Be sure the PC (tower) is plugged into a "surge protector" and that the surge protector is plugged into an electrical outlet.

2. Be sure that the monitor, the keyboard, and the mouse cables are connected to the tower.

3. Press the large button on the front of the tower and a light will come on. (The universal symbol for power is ⏻ and that symbol will be next to all power buttons or controls.)

4. Press the square button on the front of the monitor that also has the universal symbol for power ⏻.

5. Wait while the computer turns itself on—your desktop will appear in a minute or two.

6. While you wait there will be lots of messages on the monitor screen and flashing lights. This is normal. It is called "booting." Just wait.

7. If the computer "beeps" at you, read what it says and follow the instructions. Usually it says to hit "any key." That means press anything on the keyboard.

8. When you see the desktop you are ready to begin.

To Turn Off the Computer

1. Close any "open" windows by pointing the cursor on the "X" at the top right of each window. (Look at the blue title bar. It is the last of three squares.)

2. Press the Windows key (the one that looks like a flag, bottom row of keyboard).

3. Use up arrow key to go up and highlight "Shut Down."

4. Press the "Enter" key.

5. The window in front of you asks, "What do you want the computer to do?" Press the "S" key to shut down the computer or the "R" key to restart (this is also called "rebooting"). Press the "Enter" key.

6. You can also go to the Start Menu section in this chapter for additional information.

Figure 11.1 — Start Menu

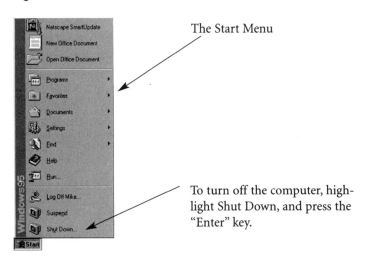

The Start Menu

To turn off the computer, highlight Shut Down, and press the "Enter" key.

Figure 11.2 — Shut Down Window

The "Shut Down" Window gives you options: You can click on OK to shut down the computer, you can restart or get Help, or you can cancel the command.

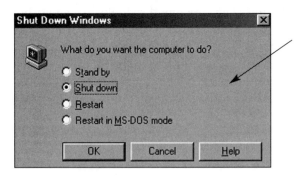

The Control Panel: How to Change Settings

The control panel includes some important items that allow you to change the default settings and customize your computer.These icons let you to make the following adjustments:

- Mouse: the speed at which the cursor (pointer) moves, its size, and how it looks (fun symbols).
- Display: the look of the desktop and windows, screen-savers, etc.
- Fonts.
- Sounds: the noises that the computer makes when it does certain tasks.
- Date and Time.

To Change the Mouse Settings

1. Press Windows key (on keyboard, looks like a flag, lowest row).

2. Use up arrow key to move up to "Settings."

3. Items like "Settings" or "Programs" will have this symbol " ▶"; this means there are more choices. Press the right arrow key to see the other items.

4. Use the right arrow key to highlight "Control Panel."

5. Press the "Enter" key to open that item.

6. Point the cursor at the icon that looks like the mouse and press the left mouse button twice (double-click).

7. The first "tab" (descriptive separator in the dialog box) is "Buttons."

   - To change to left-handed use press the "L" key.
   - To change the double-click speed, point the cursor at the slide on the timing bar and move it left or right. Check if the new speed works for you by "double-clicking" in the test box to the right.

97

8. The second tab is "Pointers." This changes the way the mouse pointer looks for different tasks. It can be fun to make changes, but I suggest waiting.

9. The third tab is "Motion."

   • To change the speed of the cursor as it moves around the desktop or a window, point the cursor at the slide on the speed track and hold down the left mouse button while dragging the slide from slow to fast.
   • To add a "trail" that will help you to see or follow the mouse as it moves around the desktop, point the cursor at the slide on the speed track and hold down the left mouse button while dragging the slide from slow to fast. Also press the "O" key or point the cursor at the white square box that says, "Show pointer trails" and press the left mouse button once (click). This activates the "trail."
   • When all is done, point the cursor at the "OK" button and press the left mouse button once (click).

10. Note that there is a special option on the control panel for the handicapped user. Point the cursor at this icon and press the left mouse button twice (double-click). Follow the directions to make any changes that you would like.

To Change Other Settings such as Display, Time and Date, and Sounds

1. Go to the icon on the control panel, open that icon by pressing the left mouse button twice (double-click), and select a "tab."

2. Go through the various choices offered and experiment in the "Test" box.

3. Make whatever changes you want.

4. Always remember to end a task by pointing the cursor at the "OK" button and pressing the left mouse button once (click).

Figure 11.4

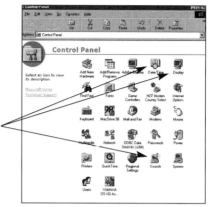

You can change the look, the time/date, and the sound your computer will make in the control panel.

How to Have Quick Access to Your Work

The reason to have items on your desktop is that it provides quick and easy access to particular programs and folders.

As an example imagine you are working on a report about chinese snuff bottles and the folder for this report is in another folder called "My Documents." You are working on this report every few days, but it does not need to stay "open" on your desktop.

1. Point the cursor on the icon "My Computer" and press the left mouse button twice (double-click).

2. Look at the window in front of you and point the cursor on the rectangle that says [C:] and double-click.

3. Look at all the folders on the C drive and point the cursor on the one named "My Documents." Press on the left mouse twice (double-click).

4. Point the cursor on the folder named "Snuff Bottle Report." Hold down the left mouse button and drag the folder out of the window and over to the left side of the desktop. Then release the left mouse button.

5. This folder is now on the desktop ready to use.

6. To open it, point the cursor on the folder and double-click.

Figure 11.5

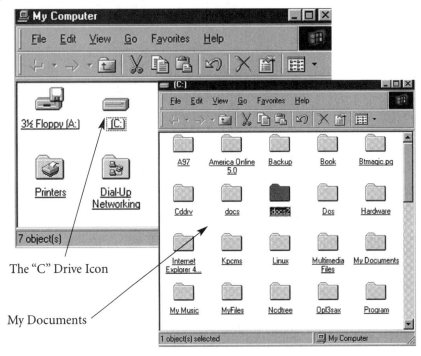

The "C" Drive Icon

My Documents

Windows: How to Open, Move, Resize, Scroll, and Close These Things!

To Open a Program or a Folder

1. Point the cursor on the folder or program icon you want and press the left mouse button twice (double-click).

2. From this window pick the files or folders that you want to open and follow the procedure above until you have the item you want.

3. Do this once more to open the window with which you want to work.

To Move a Window That Is Covering Up Something, or Just Not Where You Want It to Be

1. Point the cursor on the title bar (the blue line) at the top of the window.

2. Hold down the left mouse button and drag the window to another part of the desktop.

3. Release the left mouse button.

4. The window and everything in it will be in the new position.

To Resize a Window So It Is Easier to Work With or See

1. Point the cursor on any border around the window. The cursor will now look like a double arrow.

2. Hold down the left mouse button and drag the side or bottom of the window to the position that you want.

3. Release the left mouse button.

4. To resize a window "in proportion" (height and width), point the cursor at any corner of the window and hold down the left mouse button while dragging the box to the desired size.

5. If you do not see borders you cannot resize the window as it is already maximized.

To Scroll Down or Over in a Window to See Everything That Is There

1. If you are not seeing everything in a window, there will be a vertical light gray bar to the right and a horizontal gray bar at the bottom of the window. (See figure 11.6.)

2. Point the cursor at the up, down, right, or left arrow.

3. Hold down the left mouse button to move the contents of the screen in the desired direction.

4. You can also point the cursor anywhere along the scroll bar and press the left mouse button (click) to jump ahead to a certain area.

5. One more way to scroll is to point the cursor on the shadowed box (or rectangle) in the scroll bar. Hold down the left mouse button while dragging this box (rectangle) in the direction you want. This scrolls through long documents faster.

To Close a Window

1. Point the cursor at the "X" in the box at the top right of the window on the title bar (blue line).

2. Press the left mouse button once (click).

3. Another way to close a window:
Press the "Alt" key plus the "F4" key at the same time (Alt+F4).

4. Still one more way to close a window:
Go to the File menu (Alt+F).
Press the "C" key.
Press the "Enter" key.

Figure 11.6

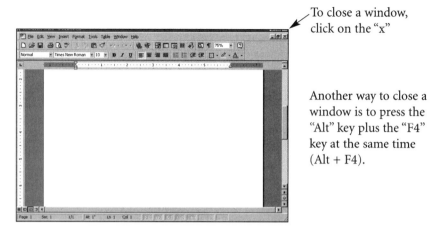

To close a window, click on the "x"

Another way to close a window is to press the "Alt" key plus the "F4" key at the same time (Alt + F4).

How to Connect with an Internet Service Provider

To Connect to America Online

1. On the desktop find the icon that says "Online Services."

2. Point the cursor on this icon and press the left mouse button twice (double-click).

3. Point the cursor at the icon that says "AOL" and double-click.

4. Instructions for setting up the service will appear on the screen. Follow them! An alternative method: if you have a CD for America Online, put the disk into your disk drive and follow the instructions.

To Connect to Another Internet Service Provider Such As Microsoft Network

Follow the instructions above, but choose a different server's icon such as "MSN." Most ISPs offer a free trial period so you might want to try several to see which works best for you. Remember you will need a different e-mail address for each ISP.

How to Receive E-Mail

1. Find the icon of your Internet Service Provider (ISP) on the left side of your desktop.

2. Point the cursor on the icon and press the left mouse button twice (double-click).

3. For America Online (AOL), look at the window in front of you and place the cursor in the box that says "Sign On." Press the left mouse button twice (double-click).

4. Wait—and wait some more while the computer's modem connects to the ISP. This can take some time, so relax.

5. Once you are connected a new window will appear.

6. If you are using AOL, a voice will say "Welcome" and will tell you if "You've got mail."

7. To read your mail, point the cursor on the icon of an open mailbox with a yellow letter in it, and press the left mouse button once (click).

8. Look at the folder and the tab that says "New Mail"—use the arrow keys to move up or down the list and "highlight" the message you want to read.

9. When you want to read the highlighted message, press the "Enter" key.

10. Read your mail!

How to Reply to E-Mail You Have Been Sent:

How to Reply to the Person Who Sent You a Message

1. Point the cursor on the icon on the right side of the message box that says "Reply" and press the left mouse button once (click). (This icon is at the top of a vertical column of icons.)

2. Note you have a new window with the "Send To" box and the "Subject" box already filled in.

3. Note that the cursor is blinking in the "message" area. (If you do not see it, press the space bar a few times and it will be more visible.)

4. Write your message.

5. Point the cursor on the icon on the right side that says "Send Now" and press the left mouse button once (click).

6. When a box appears that says "Your mail has been sent," acknowledge the computer's statement by pressing the "Enter" key or pointing the cursor on "OK" and clicking.

How to Forward the Message You Have Just Received to Someone Else

1. Point the cursor on the icon on the right side of the message box that says "Forward" and press the left mouse button once (click). (This icon is just below the "Reply" icon in the right vertical column.)

2. Note the cursor is blinking in the "Send To" box. You must fill in the recipient's e-mail address.

3. Either type in the address or go to the "Address Book" icon just below the "Forward" icon and press the left mouse button once (click).

4. Move the arrow keys up and down to highlight the name of the person to whom you want to forward the message.

5. When the correct name is highlighted press the "Enter" key.

6. To send the same message to more than one person, use the arrow keys to highlight the next name to whom you wish to send this message and press the "Enter" key.

7. Press the "Tab" key to move the cursor three times. The cursor will now be blinking in the message box. Fill in the box with a comment or note.

8. Point the cursor on the icon that says "Send Now" and press the left mouse button once (click).

9. Respond to the computer's acknowledgment that your message has been sent by pressing the "Enter" key or pointing the cursor on the "OK" button and pressing the left mouse button once (clicking).

Figure 11.7

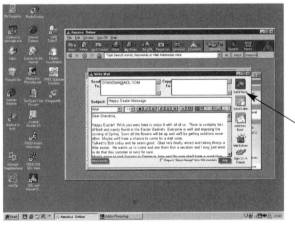

You have typed your message and are ready to send it by clicking on the "Send Now" button on the right.

How to Send Your Own E-Mail "From Scratch"!

1. There are two ways to get a "fresh piece of paper" on which to write your e-mail message.

   - With the AOL window "active," hold down the "Ctrl" key and the "M" key at the same time and then release both at the same time (Ctrl+M). Now you see a window in which you can fill in your message.

   - Find the row of icons along the third line from the top. The second one from the left looks like a piece of yellow paper. Point the cursor at the icon and press the left mouse button once (click).

2. The cursor will be blinking in the "Send To" box. Fill in the e-mail address of the person to whom you wish to send mail by typing in the address or "looking it up" in the address book.

   To fill in the address:

   - Type in the information exactly as it has been given to you. It will include a user name, the "at" symbol (@), and the name of an Internet Service Provider (example: hdl@ibm.net). Do not leave spaces or add extra punctuation. The computer is very fussy about this, unlike the postal service.

   To find the address in the address book:

   - Point the cursor on the icon that says "Address Book" in the row of vertical icons to the right of the message box and press the left mouse button once (click).

   - Use the arrow keys to find and highlight the name of the person to whom you wish to send e-mail.

   - Press the "Enter " key.

- The name should now be in the "Send To" box. Follow either procedure to add more names to the "Send To" box.

3. Press the "Tab" key to move the cursor to the next box. You probably do not need to "copy" anyone right now so press the "Tab" key again.

4. The cursor is now blinking in the "Subject" box. Fill in a few descriptive words for your recipient.

5. Press the "Tab" key again and the cursor is now in the "Message" box. Write your message.

6. When finished, point the cursor on the icon on the right that says, "Send Now" and press the left mouse button once (click).

7. Respond to the computer's notification that "Your mail has been sent" by pressing the "Enter" key or pointing the cursor on "OK" and pressing the left mouse button once (clicking).

Note: If you are *not* "signed on," the icon that says "Send Now" will be shaded and nothing will happen when you "left-click" on the icon. Your options are to click on "Send Later" or to be "on-line" when writing your mail. If you have unlimited monthly usage, this is not a problem. Otherwise you may wish to compose mail, left-click on the icon "Send Later," and the next time you are signed on, follow the procedure outlined below.

How to Send Mail in the Folder "Waiting to be Sent"

1. Compose mail "off-line." Point the cursor on "Send Later" and press the left mouse button once (click).

2. "Sign on" and wait until you are connected.

3. Press the "Alt" key and the "M" key (Alt+M) at the same time and release.

4. Use the down arrow key to highlight "Mail Waiting to be Sent,"at the bottom of the menu or press the "B" key.

5. Press the "Enter" key.

6. If you want to send the highlighted message, point the cursor on "Send" and press the left mouse button once (click).

7. Do the same for each message that you want to "Send Now."

8. If you want, send all the messages at once by clicking on "Send All"—the button all the way to the right.

Figure 11.8

To get a list of the mail you have waiting to be sent, click on Mail Center, highlight and click on Mail Waiting to be Sent, highlight the mail you wish to send, click on send.

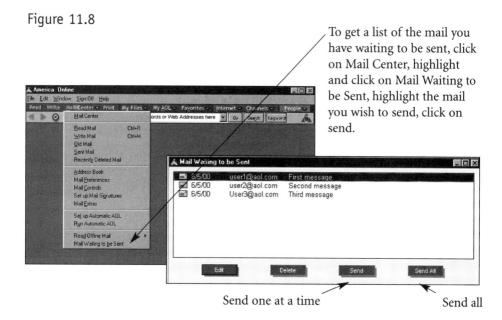

Send one at a time   Send all

How to Set Up Your Address Book

First, open America Online. On the desktop, point the cursor at the AOL icon and press the left mouse button twice (double-click).

1. Press the "Alt" key and the "M" key (Alt+M) simultaneously to bring down the "Mail Center" menu.

2. Press the "A" key to open the address book.

3. Look at lower left of window to find the icon "New Person."

4. Point the cursor on this icon and press the left mouse button once (click).

5. Fill in all the information. (Remember: move from box to box by pressing the "Tab" key.)

6. Press the "Enter" key or point the cursor on the "OK" button and click.

7. Your address book now contains this person's e-mail address.

8. Repeat this to add other names.

9. If you wish to have a group mailing find the icon "New Group":

   • Give the group a name like "All the Children" or "Women Friends."
   • Fill in each person's e-mail address in the boxes.
   • Press the "Enter" key.
   • When you wish to send something to all the children, highlight this "name" in your address book and press the "Enter" key. All the addresses of all the children will appear in the "Send To" box.

Figure 11.9

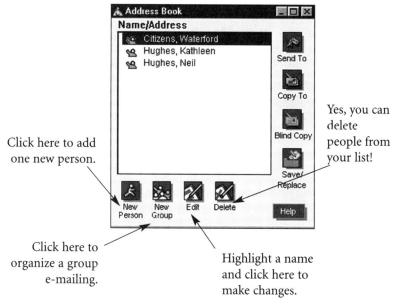

Click here to add
one new person.

Yes, you can
delete
people from
your list!

Click here to
organize a group
e-mailing.

Highlight a name
and click here to
make changes.

How to Get on the Internet

1. On the desktop, point the cursor at the AOL icon and press the left mouse button twice (double-click).

2 "Sign on" and wait until you are connected. Keep waiting— remember this could take some time!

3. On the lowest bar (fourth bar down including title bar) look for a white rectangle that says, "Type in keyword or Web address here and click GO."

4. Point the cursor in this box and press the left mouse button once to highlight the box.

5. Type:

- the name of anything you are interested in knowing more about;
- a Web address that you have gotten from an article, an advertisement, or television;
- "www." followed by the name of a company or organization and ".com" or ".org" as appropriate.

6. Press the "Enter" key.

7. Have fun! Play with whatever comes up. Click on "links" (items in blue that are underlined).

8. If you want to go back a page, point the cursor on the back arrow (on the lowest bar) and press the left mouse button once (click).

9. To Stop: point the cursor on the "X" in the upper right corner of the window and press the left mouse button once (click).

Figure 11.10

You can easily get on the Internet: "Type Keyword or Web Address here and click GO."

How to Follow the Stock Market over the Internet

Using America Online (AOL) as your ISP:

1. On the desktop, point the cursor at the AOL icon and press the left mouse button twice (double-click).

2. "Sign on" and wait until you are connected.

3. On the right side of the "Welcome" window, find the green $ icon with the word "Quotes."

4. Point the cursor on this icon and press the left mouse button once (click).

5. In the new window find "My Portfolio" (white letters on a blue/green background).

6. Point the cursor on this icon and click.

7. Go to the lower left area of the new window and find the word "Create."

8. Point the cursor on this word and click.

9. Type the name you wish to use for this portfolio in the box with the blinking cursor.

10. Press the "Enter" key.

11. Follow the directions for the next step.

12. In this new window, fill in each of the spaces as well as you can. Press the "Tab" key to move from box to box.

13. Point the cursor on the "Add Item" button and press the left mouse button once (click).

14. Repeat numbers 11-14 to add additional positions. Then click on "Next."

15. Follow directions to fill in the next step and click on "Finish."

The Start Menu

The "Start" menu is the way to "get to" *everything* in your computer. It gives you access to programs and settings, and allows you to shut down and restart your computer.

To Open This Menu

1. Press the Windows key (on keyboard, looks like a flag, lowest row).

2. Use the up arrow key to move to the item you want.

3. Items like "Settings" or "Programs" will have this symbol "▶"; this means there are more choices. Press the right arrow key to see these other choices.

4. Go up or down with the arrow keys to highlight the program or item you want to open.

5. Press the "Enter" key to open that program or item.

6. Use the arrow keys to go to the folder or item you want and highlight it.

7. Press the "Enter" key to open it.

You Can Also Use the Mouse to Do All This

1. Press the Windows key (on keyboard, looks like a flag, lowest row).

2. Point the cursor at the item you want and press the left mouse button once to highlight it (click).

3. Press the left mouse button twice to open the next menu (double-click).

4. Point the cursor on the program or item you want to open.

5. Press the left mouse button twice to open it (double-click).

6. Point the cursor on the folder or item you want to open.

7. Double-click to open it.

The Control Panel

The control panel allows you to change the default settings and customize your computer. Click on these icons to adjust the features listed.

- Mouse: the speed, size, and appearance of the cursor.
- Display: the look of the desktop and windows, screen-savers, etc.
- Fonts: the size and appearance of the typeface.
- Sounds: the noises that the computer makes when it does certain tasks.
- Date and Time.
- Printer.

Shutting Down or Restarting

1. Press the Windows key (on keyboard, looks like a flag, lowest row).

2. Use the up arrow key to highlight "Shut Down" just above Start flag.

3. Press the left mouse button once (click).

4. The desktop will be entirely shaded. Only the "Shut Down Windows" box will appear.

5. Choose whether to "Shut Down" or "Restart" and press the "Enter" key or point the cursor on the "OK" button and press the left mouse button once (click).

6. Wait for the machine to do what you have asked it to do!

7. If you shut down the computer completely, to restart it you will need to press the large button on the front of the tower with this symbol ⏻. Do not do this until the computer has been off for at least one minute (Union rules.)

8. If you restart the computer, wait for it to start itself again. It will show all sorts of words and numbers (faster then you can read them). This is "rebooting." Do not worry. When you see the desktop again you may use the machine.

Note: Usually one restarts the computer after loading a new program or changing a setting. Also when nothing seems to work (like the mouse or the keyboard), restarting is quicker and easier than shutting down the computer and letting it rest for a minute before turning it back on.

Figure 11.11

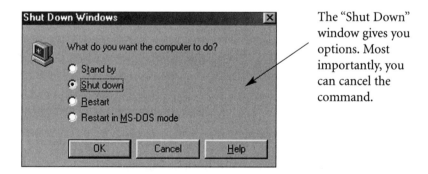

The "Shut Down" window gives you options. Most importantly, you can cancel the command.

How to Set Up Folders

1. Point the cursor on the icon on the desktop that looks like a computer and says, "My Computer."

2. Press the left mouse button twice (double-click).

3. Use the arrow keys to move to and highlight the C drive (looks like a rectangle with [C:] under it).

4. Press the "Enter" key. You can now see everything in the C drive.

5. Press the "Alt" key and the "F" key (Alt+F) simultaneously to bring down the "File" menu.

6. Press the "N" key (New).

7. Press the "F" key (Folder).

8. A yellow folder will appear. Under the folder is a box with "New Folder" written in blue. Type a name for your new folder.

9. Point the cursor on a blank area and press the left mouse button once (click).

10. To have instant access to this folder, move it to the desktop:

    • Point the cursor on the folder you want to move.
    • Hold down the left mouse button.
    • Use the mouse to drag the folder to the left side of the desktop.
    • When the folder is on the desktop, release the left mouse button.

Figure 11.12

Name the new folder
as soon as it appears
by just starting to
type a name.

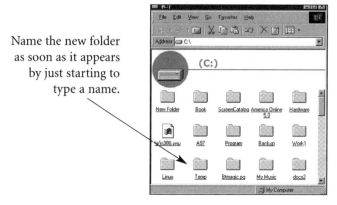

How to Create Folders in "My Documents"

1. Point the cursor on the icon that looks like an open folder and says, "My Documents."

2. Press the left mouse button twice (double-click).

3. Press the "Alt" key and the "F" key (Alt+F) simultaneously to bring down the "File" menu.

4. Press the "N" key (New).

5. Press the "F" key (Folder).

6. A yellow folder will appear. Under the folder is a box with "New Folder" written in blue. Type a name for your new folder (example: Correspondence, House, Car, Paul, Judith, Doctor-Glenda, Lawyer-Neil, Travel, etc.)

7. Point the cursor on a blank area and press the left mouse button once (click).

8. Repeat steps 3–7 to create more folders in "My Documents."

How to Move Folders

1. Open the window that contains the folder or file you want to move.

2. Point the cursor on the item you want to move and press the left mouse button once (click).

3. Press the "Ctrl" key and the "Z" key (Ctrl+Z) simultaneously to cut.

4. Open the window where you want the folder or file to go.

5. Press the "Ctrl" key and the "V" key (Ctrl+V) simultaneously to paste.

6. Everything will be moved to the new folder.

How to Write Documents, Notes, and Letters

1. Point the cursor on the icon with the "W" that says "Microsoft Word."

2. Press the left mouse button twice (double-click).

3. Look at the window in front of you. The cursor is blinking on the new "piece of paper."

4. Press the "Alt" key and the "F" key (Alt+F) to see the "File" menu.

5. Press the "A" key to show the "Save As" window.

6. Give your document a name in the lower box where the cursor is blinking.

7. Decide if you want this document to go in this folder. If not:

119

- Point the cursor on the yellow folder with an up arrow and press the left mouse button once on that folder.

- Point the cursor on the folder into which you want your document to go and press the left mouse button once on that folder.

- Check that the correct folder name is shown in the box "Save In."

8. Point the cursor on "Save" and press the left mouse button once (click).

9. Type your document.

10. Make any changes you would like (see below).

11. Pause as you type to press the "Ctrl" key and the "S" key (Ctrl+S) simultaneously about every five minutes.

12. When you are all done:

- If you want to print your work press the "CTRL" key and the "P" key (Ctrl+P) simultaneously and press the "Enter" key. (See How to Print Documents on page 124.)

- If you want to close the document, press the "Alt" key and the "F" key (Alt+F). Then press the "X" key.

- You will be asked if you want to "Save your document." Point the cursor on the "Yes" button and press the left mouse button once or press the "Y" key.

Figure 11.13

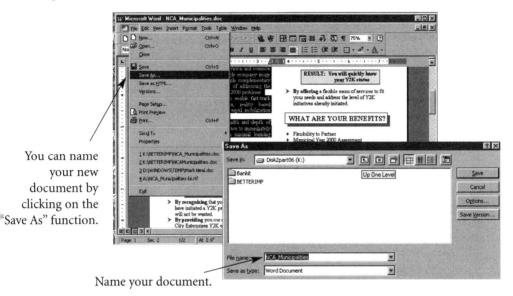

You can name
your new
document by
clicking on the
"Save As" function.

Name your document.

How To Save Documents

If you are saving a document for the first time, please read numbers
4–8 in the previous section **How to Write Documents, Notes, and
Letters**.

Keyboard Commands

1. Press the "Alt" key and the "F" key to see the "File" menu, then
   press the "S" key.
2. Press the "Ctrl" key and the "S" key at the same time (Ctrl+S).

Mouse Commands

1. Point the cursor on the icon that looks like a "floppy disk" (on
   the toolbar, third from the left) and press the left mouse button (click).

Figure 11.14

This is the
"Save"
Icon.

How to Highlight Something

1. Place the cursor at the beginning of the word, phrase, sentence, or paragraph.

2. Hold down the "Shift" key.

3. While holding down the "Shift" key, move the arrow keys until everything that you want is highlighted.

4. Release the "Shift" key.

5. To highlight the whole document: hold down the "Ctrl" key and the "A" key (Ctrl+A) simultaneously. Then release.

An Alternative Way to Highlight

1. Place the cursor at the beginning or end of item.

2. Hold down left mouse button.

3. While holding down left mouse button, drag mouse to cover the entire area to be highlighted.

4. When the area is highlighted, release left mouse button.

Still One More Way to Highlight!

1. Place cursor at the beginning of the item and press the left mouse button once (click).

2. Hold down the "Shift" key.

3. Move the cursor to the end of the item and press the left mouse button once (click).

4. Release the "Shift" key.

Change the Look of Your Document: Formatting

First type your document. Then highlight the part you wish to change. (See previous section).

To Change the Style

1. Once an area is highlighted, point the cursor at the icon that will make the change you wish and press the left mouse button once (click). (Example: "B" to make bold or "U" to underline.)

2. Point the cursor on any part of your document that is clear and press the left mouse button to "un-highlight."

To Change the Font You Are Using

1. Once an area is highlighted, point the cursor on the down arrow to the right of the name of the font (second white rectangle on format bar) and press the left mouse button once.

2. Point the cursor on the arrow of the scroll bar to the right and hold down the left mouse button to scroll down to the font you wish to use.

3. When the correct font is highlighted, press the left mouse button once (click).

4. Point the cursor on any part of your document that is clear and press the left mouse button once to "un-highlight."

To Change the Size of the Font

1. Once an area is highlighted, point the cursor on the white rectangle with a number (third from the left on the format bar).

2. Point the cursor on the down arrow and press the left mouse button once (click).

3. Point the cursor on the number of the size you wish to use and highlight it. Then click.

4. Point the cursor on any part of your document that is clear and press on the left mouse button to "un-highlight."

Figure 11.15

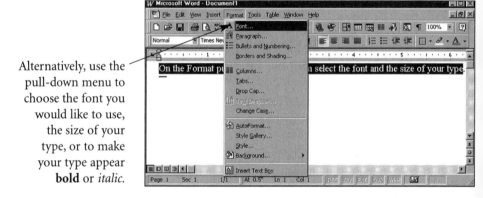

Alternatively, use the pull-down menu to choose the font you would like to use, the size of your type, or to make your type appear **bold** or *italic*.

Note: You can perform a number of these tasks *at the same time* by leaving your word or paragraph highlighted while making numerous changes. Example: highlight a sentence, change the size and style of the font, underline.

Also: If you *do not like* the changes you have made, highlight the words again and try something else or go back to the original by pressing "Undo" on the "Edit" menu or toolbar.

How to Print Documents:
Print Preview

Before printing it is best to preview your document so that you can make any changes you would like. "Print Preview" includes a tool to magnify the item and there are other tools to change margins, etc. (but you shouldn't have to change these often).

When you are ready to print your document:

1. Press the "Alt" key and the "F" key (Alt+F) to bring down the "File" menu.

2. Press the "V" key to highlight "Print Preview."

3. Press the "Enter" key.

4. Preview your document.

5. Point the cursor on the "X" on the top right of the title bar and press the left mouse button once to close the preview.

To Print Your Document

Point the cursor on the "Printer" icon (third row, fourth from left) and press the left mouse button (click).

An Alternative Way to Print

1. Press the "Ctrl" key and the "P" key (Ctrl+P) simultaneously which is the key command to print.

2. A dialog box will open. It will:

   • Confirm the printer you are using.
   • Ask what pages you want to print.

- Ask how many copies you want to print.
- Provide "Options" (for example, allowing you to print select pages rather than the entire document).

3. When you have told the machine what you want, press the "Enter" key or point the cursor on the "OK" button and press the left mouse button once (click).

Another Way to Print

1. Point the cursor on the "File" menu and press the left mouse button (click).

2. Point the cursor on "Print" and press the left mouse button (click).

3. Answer the questions in the dialog box and press the "Enter" key.

Figure 11.16

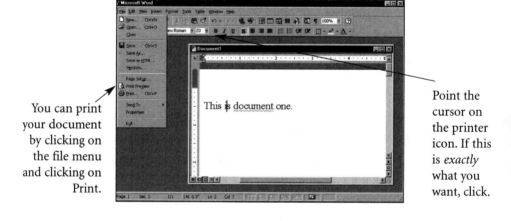

You can print your document by clicking on the file menu and clicking on Print.

Point the cursor on the printer icon. If this is *exactly* what you want, click.

How to Back Up Files:

It is important to back up (copy) your work onto a "floppy disk" so that you have an extra copy in the event that the computer really does "crash" and everything that is stored on your "hard drive" is lost.

1. Insert a disk into your floppy disk drive.

2. Follow the dialog box asking you to "OK" initializing the disk.

3. Open "My Computer" by pointing the cursor on the icon and pressing the left mouse button twice (double-clicking).

4. Point the cursor on the C drive icon and press the left mouse button twice (double-click).

5. Point the cursor on the folder that you want to "back up" and hold the left mouse button down while you drag that folder to the icon for the floppy disk (looks like a disk and says 3.5-inch floppy [A:]").

6. Release the left mouse button.

If a file is too big to be copied onto a floppy disk, an error message will appear. If this happens:

1. Open the folder you want to "back up" and move individual folders or files to the disk until it is full.

2. Then start with another disk.

LABEL EVERYTHING IMMEDIATELY! Otherwise you will forget what you put on the disk.

How to Play the Card Game Solitaire

Point the cursor at the icon on the desktop that looks like a deck of cards and says, "Solitaire." Press the left mouse button twice (double-click).(If the game is not on your desktop, see the instructions below.)

For Directions on How to Play

1. Press the "Alt" key and the "H" key (Alt+H) simultaneously.

2 Press the "H" key again.

3. Use the arrow keys to highlight the topic you want.

4. Press the "Enter" key.

To Play

1. Point the cursor on the card you want to move.

2. Hold down the left mouse button and drag the card to the column on which you want to place it.

3 Release the left mouse button.

4. To turn cards in the deck, point the cursor on the deck of cards and press the left mouse button once (click).

5. When you have run through the deck, point the cursor on the large "O" and press the left mouse button once (click).

6. Start going through the deck again.

To Play a New Game

1. Press the "Alt" key and the "G" key (Alt +G) simultaneously.

2. Press the "N" key.

3. A new game will be dealt.

To End the Game

1. Press the "Alt" key and the "G" key (Alt+G) simultaneously.

2. Press the "X" key.

3. Alternate method: point the cursor on the "X" in the upper right corner of the window and press the left mouse button once (click).

If Your Games Are Not on the Desktop

1. Go to the "Start" menu by pressing the Windows key.

2. Use the up arrow key to highlight "Programs."

3. Use the right arrow key to show the programs.

4. Use the up arrow key to go to "Accessories."

5. Use the right arrow key to show the accessories.

6. Use the arrow key to highlight "Games."

7. Use the arrow key to highlight the game you want to play.

8. Press the "Enter" key.

(Do you see why it is easier to have your games on the desktop?)

Other Games

Most card games are similar to solitaire and by going to the "Help" menu you can get instructions on how to play each one of them. Some require "clicking and dragging" and some involve just pointing the cursor and clicking.

How to Listen to CDs and Use the Volume Control

Most computers today have speakers and CD drives. If yours does not, you can purchase them.

If you place an audio CD into your CD drive, it will start to play automatically. To control what you are listening to:

1. Press the Windows key (last row on keyboard, looks like a flag).

2. Use the up arrow key to go to "Programs."

3. Use the right arrow key to see all the programs.

4. Use the up arrow key to highlight "Accessories."

5. Use the right arrow key to select "Entertainment."

6. Use the right arrow key to select "CD Player."

7. Press the "Enter" key.

8. Place a CD into the CD drive and point the cursor on whatever control you wish to use (like "Play").

9. Press the left mouse button (click) to activate the command.

To Change the Volume

1. Follow the steps above. Then press the "Alt" key and the "V" key (Alt+V).

2. Press the down arrow key, select "Volume Control" at the bottom under "CD Player."

3. Point the cursor on any of the volume control bars and hold down the left mouse button while you drag the slide to the desired position.

4. Point the cursor at the "X" on the title bar and press the left mouse button once (click) to close the window.

Figure 11.17

To change the volume, highlight and click on Volume Control to bring up the controls.

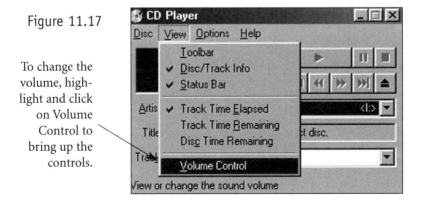

A Appendices

Appendix A
Trouble Shooting and the Usual Questions, or, Why Won't This Stupid Thing Work?

I turned on the computer, but the screen is blank.
- Did you also remember to turn on the monitor? There should be a green light on the front of the monitor to show that it is on. If it is on then perhaps you need to adjust the brightness and contrast controls. This is just like the old fashioned television! Just look around the front, side, or back and see if there is "something" that can be adjusted.

All this information is very nice, but my computer does not seem to work like this at all! What is wrong?
- Is it possible that you are using an iMac® computer made by Apple® rather than a PC? If so, you are reading the wrong book. May I suggest that you buy my companion book *The First Week with My iMac*, which should answer most of your questions.

I double-clicked on a word by mistake and it was highlighted. What do I do?
- If you want to delete the word or change something about the way it looks, you have just stumbled onto something useful. If the cursor is on a word, you can highlight that word simply by double-clicking.
- If you did *not* want to highlight that word, then just move the cursor to some other area and press the left mouse button once (click) to remove the highlight.

I double-click on an icon and nothing happens.
- Be sure you are really on the icon properly.
- If something is shaded it is "nonfunctioning." You just will not be able to do that function so stop and think why the machine doesn't want to cooperate. Example: Perhaps you have asked it to send your e-mail now, but you are not "on line" so it cannot do as you ask.

With programs and folders, how do I know when to press the left mouse button once (click) and when to press it twice (double-click)?
- Good question! It varies, but usually pressing once will highlight or select something; pressing twice will open the program. Items on the desktop usually need two "clicks." Items in programs usually will open with one "click."
- If you are in "text" it is different. Pressing the left mouse button once will place an "insertion point" at the spot where you want to do something. Pressing the left mouse button twice (double-clicking) will highlight or select that word.
- I think it's a good idea just press the left mouse button twice—it can't hurt anything and it is easier to remember.
- The key to mouse "clicking" is that you must click in the same spot each time. Also, if you want to "double-click" (press twice) you must do it quickly unless you have changed the mouse settings. If nothing happens in a short period of time, try again.

I do not remember what all the icons mean.
- If you point the cursor on an icon, a little box will drop down and tell you what that icon does.

I do not remember what the word "icon" means!
- I should tell you to go to the *Glossary*, but just this once I will answer here. An "icon" is a picture used to show certain jobs or tasks that can be performed.
- Example: If you click on the icon that looks like a printer, it sends the command to go ahead and print whatever document is currently open. The icon that looks like a check mark with "ABC" above it will check the spelling in your document if you click there.

What do all the icons on the desktop mean? When I point to them they don't provide any information.
- These icons represent programs and folders that you use a lot or that are permanently on your desktop thanks to the software manufacturers. They provide quick access to tasks you may want to do or folders that you work with all the time.

- Clicking on "My Computer" is one way of seeing everything that is in your computer. It has an icon for each of the disk drives and by opening (clicking on) one of these icons you can see all the folders in that drive. Think of it as peeling away the skin of an onion. By double-clicking on any folder it will then show you what is in that folder, and that folder, and that folder right down to the files! You can put as many folders or programs as you wish on the desktop, but try not to get carried away. The idea is to make your life less, not more, complicated.
- Also note that one of the icons looks like a wastepaper basket. That is what it is. If you do not want something just point the cursor on that file or folder, hold down the left mouse button and drag the item to the "Recycle Bin." Then release the left mouse button to throw it away.

If I put something in the Recycle Bin is it really gone forever?
- RELAX! Nothing has been lost… yet. Think of this as the beginning of the week and the trash is only picked up on Friday.
- Your document/file/folder will sit in the Recycle Bin until you "empty" it.
- To empty the Recycle Bin, point the cursor on the icon and press the left mouse button twice (double-click). LOOK AT WHAT IS THERE. Do you really want to dump it? If the answer is yes, then go to the "File" menu (Alt+F) and then press the "B" key. If you want to dump everything then press the "Enter" key.

I am holding down the "Ctrl" or "Alt" key along with another key and the computer is "binging" at me.
- After you have pressed the two keys *simultaneously*, you must *release* them *at the same time*.
- If you do not release the keys at the same time you may be giving the computer an additional key command that opens something you do not want.

I try to do something and nothing happens except the computer making a "binging" sound.
- You have asked the computer to do something it cannot do.

- Perhaps you are trying to do something before you have answered one of the computer's "questions" or the command you are trying to give is currently shaded. Stop and think why the computer doesn't want to do what you are asking.
- See if there is a window that is asking you for some response and answer the question by pressing the "Y" (yes) or "N" (no) key or pressing the "Enter" key to say "OK, that is fine."
- Perhaps you are not in an "active" window. If you try to give a command and the program is not active, the computer will "bing." Make sure the title bar (the top line) is blue.

How do I know when a program is "active"?
- You may see windows all over your desktop, but only one of them will have a blue line running along the top. This shows that this is the program that is open and "in use" or "active."

How do I get another program on the desktop to be "active"?
- All you need to do to activate a program is to "left-click" in any part of the window of a program that you see. Even if it is partially hidden, by left-clicking on anything, it will come to the front and be ready to use.
- Another way to find a "hidden" window is to look at the gray line of boxes at the bottom or top of your desktop. This is the "taskbar." It includes the symbol for the "Start" menu and to the right a row of icons with their program names. Below that line are the names and icons of all the items on your desktop. The name of any program that is sitting open on the desktop appears on the taskbar.
- To bring one of those program windows to the front as active, just left-click on the rectangle with the icon and the name of the program that you wish to use. (Left-clicking on any of the icons on the line below is the same as double-clicking on the desktop icon. It will open that program or item.)

Even with the little drop down icon names and menu information, I do not understand what all these words mean and what they do.
- Don't worry about most of the menu names and icons. The idea of this guide is a basic understanding of how to work the comput-

er. If you are ready to delve into the intricacies of "Insert," "Format," and "Tools," you are ready to buy one of the more extensive computer guides!

- However, there is no reason why you cannot experiment. I suggest that you write a paragraph on any subject. Then try highlighting a line and press the icon that looks like scissors on the line below the title bar (blue line). The highlighted line is "cut out"! Next, point the cursor in the middle of some other line, left-click, and then go up to the icon line and click on the icon that looks like a clipboard. The line that you cut out should be there now.
- The idea is just to press different things and see what happens!

What do I do when I make a mistake and press the wrong key and half my letter disappears?

- Look at the icon bar (the third line at the top of your screen). In the fourth section there are two curved arrows, one points backward and one points forward. The first will "Undo" what you've just done; the second will "Redo" your last action. (For fun, just click on each of these icons and watch your edit appear and disappear.)
- Alternatively, go to the "Edit" menu by either pointing the cursor on the word "Edit' and left-clicking or pressing the "Alt" key and the "E" key simultaneously (Alt+E). Now press the "U" key to "Undo" the cut that you just made.
- To be on the safe side, it's best to click on the "Undo" icon or word "Undo" from the "Edit" menu immediately after making a mistake. With some word-processing programs, if you wait and do even one thing, you cannot undo your previous mistake. Other programs let you undo a number of previous actions.

Why does everyone make such a fuss about "saving" things?

- Saving your work as you go along is a way of ensuring that all your hard work is not lost. We have all forgotten to do this and "paid the price" by having hours of work disappear, forever. It is not fun when this happens! "Saving" can save you a lot of unhappiness.

i WAS TYPING ALONG AND SUDDENLY EVERYTHING WAS cAPITAL LETTERS except FOR THE THINGS I WANTED TO MAKE cAPITAL!
- You have pressed the "Caps Lock" key by mistake or left it on by mistake. When this happens, just press the "Caps Lock" key again and it will unlock.
- You can see when the "Caps Lock" key is turned on as there is a light on the keyboard that goes on when this feature is in use. (Think of the high beams of your car lights. You do not realize they are on until it is pointed out to you. Then you look at the dashboard and you see that the blue light is on.)

I left out a letter in a word and when I went back to put it in, the next letter disappeared! What happened and why are all the letters getting lost?
- On the right side of your keyboard, above the arrow keys, there are a group of keys with words on them. One of the keys says "Insert." What it does is to insert a letter or name while taking out whatever was "in" that space. This key was activated by mistake. That is why your other letters were lost.
- You can tell if the "Insert" key is active by looking at the line at the bottom of your window (below your "piece of paper"). On this gray line you have lots of information including what page you are working on and what line you are typing. (I am watching these numbers change as I type these words and it is a lot of fun!) There are five boxes with letters that are shaded when nothing is active. If something like the "Insert" key is active, the appropriate box will be highlighted.

I only wanted one word to be underlined/ italicized/ bold and now all the words that follow are like that. How do I get back to normal?
- You changed font and the computer did not know that you wanted to change only a portion of the text. When you have completed the section you are working on, you need to change back to the original font.
- Look at the format bar and notice that the "**B**" or "*I*" or "U̲" has a box around it. This means that it is active. Before typing your

next word or line, point the cursor on the appropriate letter and left-click. It is no longer active and everything will be normal.
- Another way to get everything back to normal is to look at the white rectangle all the way to the left. It should say "Normal" and you should then see the font that you want to see in the size that you would like. Change these settings if they are not as you wish.
- When all else fails, you can go to the "Edit" menu and press the letter "U" to undo what you have done. The key command for this is Ctrl+Z.

What do all the lines and numbers mean at the bottom of the window when I am writing something?
- These numbers tell you what page you are working on and other details such as the line you are on, the number of pages in your document, and whether any special features are in use such as the "Insert" key. (See above.)

How do I change the way the typing looks?
- To change the font you need to highlight the word/phrase/sentences you want to change and then use the tools on the format bar to make changes. DO NOT FORGET: whatever you want to change must be highlighted.
- If you change the look of a section and then decide you do not like it just remember "Undo" in the "Edit" menu.

I tried to give a new file a name and the machine makes a noise and will not let me do it. What is the problem?
- In Windows 98 you can have a file name that is hundreds of characters and spaces long. In Windows 95 you can only have 32 characters and spaces. (This means that you can have a file name such as Lawyer-Jonathan-Wills and Trusts, but you cannot use the complete name of his law firm!)
- However there are certain characters that you cannot use because of old conventions from other computer languages. These are the forward and back slash (/) and (\), the colon and asterisk (:) and (*), the bar and angle brackets (I) and (< >), and the question mark (?).

Can I mix clicking the mouse button with using key commands?
- Yes. Sometimes it is easiest to point the cursor and left-click when you are using the mouse a lot. At the same time there is no reason you cannot use "Alt" + "T" to bring down the tools menu and then use the mouse to highlight and select the tool you want, like "Spell Check."

Why can't I use the right mouse button?
- BECAUSE I SAID SO! (I have been waiting for this question....) Actually the right mouse button is very important and is a wonderful shortcut to all sorts of information. It will call up a menu with a set of actions from which to choose.
- IT IS ALSO SOMETHING YOU DO NOT NEED RIGHT NOW. It will only confuse you and you also might make some big mistakes that will delete or lose things in your computer, like some of your programs!

How do I get rid of a window that I don't want to use?
- To get rid of a window you can either:
  1. Point the cursor on the box with an "X" in it at the top right of your window and click on it with the left mouse button, or
  2. Press the "Alt" key + "F" key and when the file menu drops down just press the "X" key to "Exit," or
  3. Press the "Ctrl" key and "F4" key simultaneously.
- However if it is not a "window" but rather a dialog box, then you need to answer the question you are being asked before you can continue your work.

How do I get rid of the screen-saver my child/friend added to my desktop?
- To change the "look" of your desktop you need to go to the "Start" menu, highlight "Settings," highlight "Control Panel" and open it.
- Double-click on "Display." You now can make all sorts of changes. (For more detailed instructions go to Chapter 11.)

How do I get rid of a child or grandchild (the one that is giving me more information than I can absorb)?

- I suppose they are too old and too jaded to accept $1.00 to go out for ice cream?
- No, really. You have to be honest with them. Tell the person that you appreciate what they are trying to tell you, but you just are not following it right now. Suggest that it would be better to go over this when you are not so tired/hungry/preoccupied/overwhelmed.
- **This is important:** Do not have someone come to help you when you are not ready to listen and follow directions. It will make you unhappy and it will be very frustrating for the person trying to teach you. This is especially true when talking to your children on the telephone. I have a basic "three-strike rule." If we have tried to do something three times, unsuccessfully, it is time to stop! There is nothing wrong with saying, "Not now, thank you" or "This is not a good time!" or "Let's try this again tomorrow." (I have said it to my mother and she has said it to me—and we are still talking to each other!)

Everything stopped working! I cannot get the mouse to move or any of the keys to work. What do I do?

- This happens to my mother all the time! The first thing to do is to check that the keyboard and the mouse are still plugged in. It is possible that if you have been sliding things around that they have been disconnected. You need to make sure that the wires are pushed all the way in. Now try the mouse or control keys again.
- If this is not the problem, then the easiest thing to do is to turn off the computer by pressing the button on the tower that is lit. (Or if you have a "reset" button, press it once. (Check your owner's manual for location). WAIT ONE FULL MINUTE. Then press the power button again to restart the computer.
- The computer will go through all its start-up procedures and will probably tell you that it is unhappy that you shut it down improperly. It will tell you that it is checking everything to make sure it is OK. It might ask you to press "any key" to start this process. Do this. Press one of the keys on the keyboard–it makes no difference which one! Then just wait and in a minute you will see the desktop again.

How do I know when to use the "Alt" key and when to use the "Ctrl" key?

- The "Alt" key is normally used with another key to bring down a menu. However it also works on its own. Pressing the "Alt" key all by itself will place you at the beginning of the menu bar.
- The "Ctrl" key can be used to issue direct commands without first going to a menu. For example, you can have the computer print your work by pressing the "Ctrl" key and the "P" key. You did not have to first go to the menu bar or the "Print" icon. If you do go to the menu bar you will see that this command is shown on the right side of the menu (next to "Print"). Another example is saving, which can be done by pressing the "Ctrl" key and the "S" key simultaneously.

Why should I be interested in going to some of the Web sites you mention?

- I have given a number of interesting Internet addresses to help start you out. I have tried most of these myself and thought they were either informational or funny.
- I also think that by trying some of these sites, you will understand the breadth and depth of the Internet and become aware of many things you did not realize were available.
- For an example, I suggest going to the National Public Radio Web site, www.npr.org.
  1. When you get to the home page, go down to radio shows and select "All Thing Considered."
  2. If you want to see what is on today, that is fine. Otherwise, click on "Archives" and pick one of last week's programs.
  3. Scroll through the list of reports for the day and notice that they also show what musical selections were played.
  4. Pick one of the reports and click on the "link" (the blue words).
  5. Now wait. In a moment another window will open and you will actually hear the report that was broadcast over the air! You never have to worry about missing an item on this show!
- What I have suggested for National Public Radio can also be done for other radio stations and several television news networks. Just try it for fun!

How do I program my VCR so that the clock stops blinking at me?
- For that answer you will need to buy my next book: *My VCR, My Friend.*

If I am asking all these questions, should I consider moving on to a more advanced instruction book?
- Sure, why not? After all this is a very basic guide. Now that you know how to get everything "up and running," you will feel a lot more comfortable following some of the other computer books. It will also be easier to think of your question and find an answer using another book's index. Enjoy!

To wrap things up, here's the number one question that is asked when people call the technical support line at one of the largest computer companies in the world:

Where is the "Any" key? I cannot find it on the keyboard!
- This question arises from a prompt in the start-up process that says to "Press any key to continue." I am not making this up. People actually do ask the tech support people to tell them where this key is on their keyboard. The company is rewriting their software to say, "Press the 'Enter' key." So you see, you really should not worry about asking a stupid question. Most of them have already been asked.

Appendix B
Some Important Key Commands

Basic Functions

Copy	"Ctrl" + "C"
Cut	"Ctrl" + "X"
Find	"Ctrl" + "F"
New Document	"Ctrl" + "N"
Open	"Ctrl" + "O"
Paste	"Ctrl" + "V"
Print	"Ctrl" + "P"
Repeat Typing	"Ctrl" + "Y"
Save	"Ctrl" + "S"
Select All	"Ctrl" + "A"
(highlight whole document)	
Undo Typing	"Ctrl" + "Z"

Opening Menus

Edit Menu	"Alt" + "E"
File Menu	"Alt" + "F"
Format Menu	"Alt" + "O"
(fonts, etc)	
Help Menu	"Alt" + "H"
Tools Menu	"Alt" + "T"
(spell check, etc)	

Formatting

Highlight the text, then:

Bold	"Ctrl" + "Shift" + "B"
Italics	"Ctrl" + "Shift" + "I"
Underline	"Ctrl" + "Shift" + "U"

E-mail

To write mail	"Ctrl" + "M"
(America Online)	

Appendix C
Some "World Wide Web" Addresses of Interest

Please note: I neither endorse nor suggest that you use any of these addresses. They are included as a "starting off" point to help get you involved with the Internet and to show you how logical the "addresses" are. Many popular magazines, newspapers, and television shows announce new and interesting sites all the time. Be prepared to copy down anything that sounds interesting to you.

Search Engines

Altavista	www.altavista.com
Ask Jeeves	www.askjeeves.com
Google	www.google.com
Northernlight	www.northernlight.com
Snap	www.snap.com
Yahoo	www.yahoo.com

General Information

Weather

The Weather Channel	www.theweatherchannel.com
National Weather Service	www.noaa.gov

News

Newsweek Magazine	www.newsweek.com
Time Magazine	www.time.com
CNN	www.cnn.com
CNN Video Select (video news clips)	www.cnn.com/videoselect
MSNBC (cable TV station)	www.msnbc.com
National Public Radio	www.npr.com
British Broadcasting Company	www.bbc.co.uk

Education

Smithsonian Institution (museums)	www.si.edu
Library of Congress (everything)	http://lcweb.loc.gov/library/
New York Public Library (almost everything)	www.nypl.org
Encyclopedia Britannica (charge)	www.eb.com
The Encyclopedia Mythica (mythology)	www.pantheon.org/mythica
Language	www.wordsmith.org
American Sign Language	www.hoh.org/~mastertech/asldict.spml
For Women	www.ivillage.com

Services

Postage and Zip codes	www.usps.gov
Postage	www.stamps.com
Finding people	www.switchboard.com

Health

Directories

U.S. Dept. of Health and Human Services	www.healthfinder.com
National Library of Medicine (NIH)/medlineplus	www.nlm.nih.gov/medlineplus.com
Mayo Clinic	www.mayohealth.com

Organizations

American Heart Association	www.americanheart.org
American Diabetes Association	www.diabetes.org
American Association of Retired People	www.aarp.org
Linking Human Systems (physical, mental, and addictions)	www.linkinghumansystems.com

Nutrition and Food

Tufts University	www.navigator.tufts.edu
Internet Chef	www.ichef.com/ichef-recipes/
(30,000 recipes)	
Recipes	www.epicurious.com

Alternative Medicine   www.altmedicine.com

Pharmacy   www.drugstore.com

Fitness Link   www.fitnesslink.com

Travel

Tickets, etc.

Travel information	www.travelocity.com
Travel and more	www.priceline.com
Travel and tickets	www.expedia.com
More ideas	www.smarterliving.com

Maps

Maps and driving instructions	www.mapblast.com
Another map service	www.expediamaps.com
Still one more	www.mapquest.com

Restaurants

Fodor's restaurant index   www.Fodors.com

Entertainment

Movies

Internet Movie Data Base	www.imdb.com
Reviews	www.moviefone.com

Books

Barnes & Noble	www.barnesandnoble.com
Books, music, and more	www.amazon.com
More books	www.bookfinder.com
Book news, reviews, etc.	www.bookwire.com
Comparison of prices	www.bestbookbuys.com

Music

Directory	www.listen.com
General	www.mp3.com
Lyrics	www.lyrics.ch/index.htm.com
Software	www.real.com

Sports

General	www.sportsline.com
General	www.espn.com
Statistics	www.rotonews.com

Shopping, Games, and Toys

Connection to many stores	www.shopnow.com
Comprehensive shopping resource	www.buy.com
Connection to buy gift certificates	www.giftcertificates.com
Toy shopping	www.etoys.com
Chocolate in every way	www.chocolatepicture.com
Auctions	www.ebay.com
More auctions	www.artnet.com
Download software	www.shareware.com
More software	www.download.com
Games	http://games.yahoo.com
Shopping search engine	www.piig.com

This site is a different approach to finding things on the Web. Type in www.p(whatever you are interested in)q.com (example: pbooksq.com) and it will take you directly to online stores in your area of interest.

Important: If you are buying something on the Internet there are four things to remember:

1. Make sure it is a "Secure Site," which means there should be a little icon that looks like a closed padlock visible;
2. Always pay by credit card as you will only be liable for a maximum of $50 if something goes wrong;
3. Only give your credit card number and billing/shipping address— no personal information that is not required; and
4. Ask about their return policy.

Finance

General Information
Wall Street Journal	www.wsj.com
More information	www.thestreet.com
Still another site	www.fool.com

Taxes
Advice	www.taxprofet.com
Planning	www.irs.ustreas.gov
More advice	www.fairmark.com

Computer Information

PC Magazine	www.pcmag.com
PC World	www.pcworld.com
General information on everything	www.cnet.com
Shopping	www.onsale.com
More shopping	www.edw.com

Unusual and Interesting

Blue Mountain   www.bluemountain.com
Free electronic greeting cards for every occasion and in several
languages. A great way to send some cheer.

United Nations   www.hungersite.com
World Food Program
A way to give food to a starving person at no cost to yourself. Each
log-on provides a single serving of food; one log-on a day is
permitted. "Bookmark" this site. Make a difference!

Kooponz.com   www.kooponz.com
Money-saving coupons for you to print and clip—good in 44 states.

Another site for   www.coolsavings.com
money-saving coupons

Outletzoo   www.outletzoo.com
Clearance shopping site where prices drop as time goes on!

Duct Tape   www.octane.com/ducttape.html
(everything you want to know!)

A World of Tea   www.stashtea.com
(history and more)

Birds   www.birder.com
(a megasite for bird-watchers)

SETI   www.setiathome.ssl.berkeley.edu
(Search for Extra-Terrestrial Intelligence)
A way to help scientists and a great screen-saver.

Appendix D
E-Mail Etiquette: "Smileys," Abbreviations, and Other Tips

You may or may not have heard the term "shouting." It refers to a message sent in ALL CAPITAL LETTERS. This is very annoying. It is also difficult to read. *Do not* type your messages using all capital letters as it is considered rude!

You may have heard the term "flaming." To "flame" someone is to send them an insulting or angry message. This is also something that is considered rude. If you are really that angry with someone you know, then call him or her up on the telephone and straighten it out. If you do not know the person to whom you are sending angry messages over the Internet, why are you getting so upset with a stranger?

"Smileys" (also called "emoticons") are a combination of keyboard characters that express a feeling. They use colons, semicolons, apostrophes, dashes, parentheses, and letters to make (sideways) "faces." (When you try to type some of these symbols into a Word document, the program will automatically change the characters to a graphic symbol, but in an e-mail message the characters stay as they are typed.) Some people like to include them in their messages, so here are some examples.

Smile	:-)
Frown	:-(
Indifferent	:-I
Cry	:'-(
Wink	;-)
Laugh	:-D
Kiss	;-x
Shocked	:-o
Screaming	:-@
Angry	>:I

E-mail abbreviations are a type of shorthand using the first letter of each word in a phrase to convey a thought. It saves time typing out these phrases and many people already use the abbreviations in everyday speech. An example is saying "ASAP" rather than "As Soon As Possible." Other examples include:

FYI	For Your Information
LOL	Laugh Out Loud
IRL	In Real Life
B4N	Bye for Now
F2F	Face to Face
CUL8R	See You Later
ROTFL	Rolling on the Floor Laughing
IMO	In My Opinion
IMHO	In My Humble Opinion (rarely meant that way!)
IOW	In Other Words
BTW	By the Way
WRT	With Respect to
FAQ	Frequently Asked Question
RSN	Real Soon Now
GMTA	Great Minds Think Alike
TIA	Thanks in Advance
BRB	Be Right Back
AWTTW	A Word to the Wise
PD	Public Domain
RL	Real Life

Appendix E
Tech Support: Phone Numbers and
Web Site Addresses

While this is a very useful guide in many ways, the fact is that
everyone needs to call Tech Support for help every now and then.
Do not be afraid to do this. The people at the other end of the phone
are wonderful and patient. They also want to be helpful. Just recognize
that you may have to wait *a very long time* to get someone on the line
to help you. For this reason you should have food, drink, and a book or
a project to work on within reach before placing the telephone call.

Computer Companies

Acer	1-800-637-7000	www.acer.com
Compaq	1-800-652-6672	www.compaq.com
Dell	1-800-642-9896	www.dell.com
Gateway	1-800-846-2301	www.gateway.com
Hewlett Packard	no toll free number	www.hp.com/go/support
IBM	1-800-237-5511	www.ibm.com
Micron	1-800-209-9686	www.micronpc.com
Toshiba	1-800-999-4273	www.csd.toshiba.com

Software Companies

Adobe	1-408-536-6000	www.adobe.com
Corel	1-800-772-6735	www.corel.com
FileMaker Corp	1-415-382-4700	www.filemaker.com
Intuit	1-650-944-6000	www.intuit.com
Lotus	1-978-988-2500	www.lotus.com
Microsoft	1-425-882-8080	www.microsoft.com
Symantec–Norton	1-800-441-7234	www.symantec.com

Appendix F
Healthy Computer Habits: Taking Care of Yourself Physically and Mentally

As I mentioned before, it is very easy to become enamoured of your computer. Before you know it you have spent a whole evening "surfing the Web" or playing games. Perhaps you are enjoying the "Word" program so much that you are writing your own book! You may be familiar with terms like "ergonomics," "carpal tunnel syndrome," and "Internet addiction." However, you see no reason why any of this would apply to you—after all, you are just a beginner and not really *"working"* at the computer. If you believe this, you are *wrong!* On a serious note, I strongly urge you to read the section below and follow the advice given.

Your Physical Well-being
While we have discussed "setting-up" your computer, we have not discussed how you should position yourself in front of the computer. This gets into ergonomics, the science concerned with the safe and efficient interaction of people and machines. Here are some things you need to check and do so that you sit comfortably and do not injure yourself while using the computer.

Position
You must sit squarely in front of the keyboard and monitor—not at an angle. The keyboard should be at a height that allows your elbows to bend at a 90-degree angle. You do not want to have "cocked" wrists. Position yourself in the chair so that when you look straight ahead at your monitor, your eyes are focused on the center of the screen.

You should have your chair at a height that allows your feet to rest on the floor (use a little footstool if necessary—the best type is sloped). Try not to lean forward with your chin pushing out.

Make sure your keyboard is comfortable for you. There are several styles and one might "fit" your hands or size better than the one you have. There are several types of "mice" as well. Go to a computer store and test a few to see if there is one that's easier for you to use.

Exercises

Every 20 minutes STOP WHAT YOU ARE DOING! It is very important to get up and move around a bit. Place your two hands together with the palms touching and the fingers pointed up. Now slide your hands down, holding the palms together so that you feel the stretch in your wrists. Roll your wrists in a circular motion. (Yes, both directions—let's stay balanced!)

Place your left wrist on your right forearm and press down with the wrist while pressing up with your arm. Now put your right wrist on your left forearm and do the same thing.

Drop your head down a bit and let your chin tuck back toward your neck. Now place your fingers on your chin and gently press your chin back with your fingers while you push your chin forward.

While sitting in a chair, raise your legs off the floor so that your feet are not touching the ground. Now rotate your ankles in such a way that it is as if you are using your feet to "write" the alphabet. Go through the whole alphabet twice. (This exercise is not really that important for your work on the computer, but it is a great exercise to keep your ankles strong and it is easy to do anywhere!)

Go get a drink of water. You need eight glasses a day anyway and it will clear your head for the work you are doing.

For Those Who Wear Bifocals

It is important to understand that the computer screen is a new and interesting distance from your face. You are looking at a machine that is further away than a book, but closer than the television. Go to your eye doctor and explain that you are now using a computer. He or she will make a lens the right focal distance and similar to the reading portion of your bifocals. This means you will not have to tilt your head back, injuring your neck, in order to use the tiny reading circle on standard bifocals.

Your Mental Well-being

Earlier in the book, I made a joke about naming your computer. I suggested that giving the machine a "name" would personify it and cause you to spend more time with it. The reality is that for some people, spending time on the computer does become an obsession. It has been recognized by authorities and given a name: Internet addiction.

Again you may think that you are only a beginner and can barely "sign on" let alone spend your days and nights playing games or "looking up things." The reality is that it is just as easy to become addicted to this form of entertainment as any other such as gambling, drugs, exercise, sex, etc. There are many people who literally forget to eat and sleep because they are totally immersed in their machine. On a personal note, I have already told you that I spent hours each night trying to "beat" the computer at solitaire while visiting my mother and setting up her computer. When I start a writing project, it is very difficult for me to remember to pick up my son at school or to even stop to go to the bathroom!

It is for this reason that I warn you about this issue. It is a serious problem for many people. I have included a Web site address that will be useful to you if you or anyone you know might have a problem with addictions. It is a group called Linking Human Systems™. This is an organization that helps families by guiding them through intervention and therapy. It has one of the highest success rates in the country in helping all ages and types of "substance" abusers get the help they need. It is also a resource for consultation and counseling on health issues, both mental and physical. If you have any concerns about your own behavior or that of anyone in your family, you might want to go "on-line" and see what they can do for you (www.linkinghumansystems.com).

G Glossary

This glossary includes more words and terms than you would normally expect in a book on basic computers. In fact, there are some words that you will not find in the body of this book. I chose to include additional information as you might be reading articles or hearing terms that you do not understand. My thought is that this glossary can be a resource to you well past the first week.

A: The identifier used to show the first disk drive, which is the "floppy disk drive." This is the drive that the operating system always checks for start-up instructions. It then checks the C drive, which is the hard disk drive.

Access time The amount of time it takes for data to arrive at a particular place after it has been requested.

Accessories Mini-programs that come as part of your Windows 98® operating system. Examples: a calculator, games, Notepad, Paint, and Wordpad.

Active desktop A feature of Windows 98® that allows you to view Web pages and mini-programs directly on your desktop. Mini-programs include such things as a stock ticker, a weather map, a nd a clock.

Active window The window that is currently in use on your desktop, and the window that contains the cursor. You can recognize it by the title bar which is a horizontal blue bar at the top of the window with white letters describing the window. (If the window is not active, then the bar is light gray with dark gray letters.) Only one window can be active at a time.

Address The exact location on a disk where information (a file) is stored. Addresses are used to find files on your computer and on the Internet. (On the Internet, addresses are also called URLs.)

Application Another word for program. It is software that does a particular task.

Arrow 1. An icon that appears on the desktop and is controlled by, and shows where, the mouse is moving. 2. Keys on the keyboard that look like arrows and move the cursor (or insertion point) one place at a time in the direction indicated.

ASCII The acronym for American Standard Code for Information Interchange (pronounced "askee"). This is the standard code system that allows different computers to "talk" to each other by assigning numeric values to every letter, number, symbol, etc.

"Backspace" key A key on the upper right side of the keyboard that moves the cursor one space to the left. As it does this, it erases one character at a time.

Backup A copy of data files or programs that you create as insurance in case there is an accident and your original is damaged or lost.

Bit The basic or smallest unit of measurement for electronic data. It is a contraction of BInary digiT, and it stands for 0 (on) or 1 (off). When eight bits are combined it makes a unit called a "byte." Computers can combine "0"s and "1"s to represent every letter, number, and punctuation mark.

Boot To start the computer. The computer uses information that it has stored in its own section of the hard drive to "restart" itself. It then loads the rest of the operating system into memory. The term comes from the idea that the computer is "pulling itself up by its own bootstraps."

Bounce A term used when e-mail is returned to the original sender because it could not be delivered due to an error. For example, if a message is undeliverable because of an incorrect address.

Browser A program that gives you access to the Internet and helps you to easily retrieve information from the World Wide Web.

Bug An error in the hardware or software of the computer. If it is in the software, changes must be made to the program. If it is in the hardware, then it is a real mess, as new circuits must be made and installed.

Button An element that is part of a GUI (see *Graphical User Interface*) and lets you select an option from a dialog box, a bar, etc.

Byte The amount of space needed to represent a single character (eight bits). As this is a very small unit and many bytes are needed to handle a word-processing program, terms for larger units have developed such as "kilobyte," "megabyte," and "gigabyte" (1 billion bytes).

C: The identifier usually applied to the first hard disk drive.

Cache A folder for temporarily storing frequently used files in a special area on your computer. In effect, it speeds up the operation of the computer for those tasks performed most often.

"Cancel" button An element in a dialog box, which is a GUI (See *Graphical User Interface*). Pressing this button allows you to cancel an operation or move to the next higher level of a program.

Carpal tunnel syndrome A form of wrist and hand injury caused by repetitive movements such as typing. It is important to have an ergonomic position while seated at the computer, and to take frequent breaks while typing in order to avoid this problem.

Cascade A way of arranging overlapping windows so that you can see the blue title bar and the left side of each window as they are stacked one on top of the other.

Cascading menus A set of menus and sub-menus that appear when you select certain pull-down menu commands.

CD-ROM An acronym for "compact disk read-only memory." A CD-ROM is a high-capacity storage device that can hold up to 650 megabytes of data, which is the equivalent of the information on 500 floppy disks or 300,000 pages of text. The information on the disk is permanent and cannot be changed.

CD-ROM drive A special computer disk drive that reads CDs. Depending on how many drives the computer has, it can be the D, E, F, G, or H drive.

CPU An acronym for "Central Processing Unit." This controls the computer and handles the main processing. It is commonly referred to as a "chip." (See *Pentium®*.)

Check boxes These are square boxes within dialog boxes that allow you to select or deselect your choices by clicking (or toggling on and off). The selection is "on" when a check mark appears. Often you can select more than one option.

Chip An integrated circuit.

Circuit board The board on which chips are mounted. The main circuit board of a computer is often referred to as the "motherboard."

Click To press and release a mouse button quickly in order to make a selection. It usually refers to pressing the left mouse button once. If the right mouse button is to be pressed, the command will usually say, "right-click."

Clipboard The place where information is temporarily held after it has been copied or clipped from a document. This information can then be transferred to another location.

Close button The button with an "X" on the top right of the title bar of a window. You can click this button to close a window.

Closing a window This means that you are removing the contents of a window from memory and from the screen. It is important to "save" your work, otherwise all the data will be lost when you close the window. If you close an application window it means you have stopped working in that program.

163

Command button An element in a dialog box that carries out a specific action. Examples of command buttons are the "Cancel" button and the "OK" button.

Control menu The icon on the left edge of the title bar of each application that gives a menu with a variety of options, including ways to reshape the size of the window, etc.

Control panel A folder in Windows that shows hardware applications and allows you to change the settings and options for both hardware and software, thus adjusting many systems features.

Crash An unexpected stoppage while working on some task or program. The computer does not respond to any key or mouse commands. It is caused by a failure or error of either the software or hardware. A computer virus can also cause a crash. If this occurs, you will probably have to "reboot" (restart) your computer. If you have not backed-up or saved your work, it might be lost in a system crash.

"Ctrl" key ("Control" key) A key that is found on the lowest row of the keyboard on both the left and right side. It is used in combination with other keys as a shortcut to tell the computer to do various tasks.

Cursor A special character on the desktop or in an application that shows where the next character will appear when something is typed. It can be controlled or moved by the arrow keys on the keyboard or by moving the mouse to the desired spot and clicking. The cursor changes shape as it moves around the screen, indicating when it can perform different tasks. (When working with text it is also called the "insertion point" and it blinks.)

D: The identifier usually applied to a second hard disk drive or to the CD drive.

Data Information in a form that the computer can use for processing.

Database Any collection of related information or "objects" (reports, forms, tables, etc.) created, organized, and controlled by a database management system.

Data file A file containing information.

Default The standard or predefined setting. It is used if you specify no other setting.

Delete To get rid of something. When you delete a folder it goes to the "recycle bin" and it stays there until it is purged or restored.

Desktop An on-screen version of a desktop that shows windows, icons, files, and accessories that you use to do your work. It is what you see first after you start your PC and are ready to use the computer. It is best thought of as your "work space."

Dialog box A window that appears on the screen to ask you for more information or to confirm an action you wish to take. You must respond to this "computerized questionnaire" before the program will continue. (See *Button* and *Check box.*)

Dimmed command A command that is not available to you at this time. It is shown in light gray rather than black.

Disc An alternate spelling for "disk" that usually refers to a CD. (In the interest of consistency, "disk" is used throughout this book.)

Disk A magnetic surface that permanently stores information. The internal hard disk of most computers holds most of your information. Removable disks such as "floppy disks" or "zip disks" are used to back up, or save, data from the hard disk.

Disk drive The mechanism that reads and writes information from and to a disk. There are several types of disk drives: floppy disk drives, hard disk drives, zip disk drives, compact disk drives, etc.

Display Another word for monitor.

Document A file that you create when you save work in an application program.

Domain (and domain name) A means of identifying computers at a location on the Internet. In the United States, the "domain" is the last three letters of an Internet address. It tells you with what kind of group you are communicating. Examples of domains are: .com (a commercial organization), .org (a nonprofit organization), .edu (an educational institution), .gov (part of the U.S. government), and .net (a network). The "domain name" is an easily recognizable name given to a "host" computer rather than using a numerical address.

Double-click To press the left mouse button quickly two times. This is done to select an object or program and open it.

Download To copy files from one computer to another using a network connection. Usually this refers to copying files from the Internet onto your hard drive.

Dragging Moving something, such as a folder, by holding down the left mouse
button and sliding the mouse over until the object is in the desired position on the screen. It also refers to holding down the mouse button and moving the mouse in order to highlight a string of text.

Drop-down list A list of items in a dialog box that gives possible alternatives from which to choose.

Electronic Mail (See *E-mail.*)

E-mail A way of sending messages electronically from one person to another over the Internet or a network. Messages are sent almost instantly and can contain text, files, voice messages, graphics, and photographs. It is a means of communicating around the world at great speed.

Emoticon A set of characters used to visually express an emotion.

Also known as "smileys," emoticons are commonly used in e-mail messages.

"Esc" key ("Escape" key) A key found on the top left side of the keyboard that is used to cancel an activity or process. When you want to stop an operation, this is the quick way to do it.

Extensions Short last "names" on the end of file names that help identify what program created the file. Examples include: .
- .doc—A Word document.
- .tiff—Tagged Image Format. A graphics file.
- .nf—Rich Text Format. A file that can be transmitted to other application programs without losing its format.
- .jpg—Joint Photographic Exeperts Group. A compressed file of photo images or scanned pictures.

FAQ The acronym for "frequently asked questions."

Field A place in a record for one piece of information.

File An collection of information, such as a document, that is stored on a disk.

File extension (see *Extension*)

File format (see *Extension*)

Floppy disk A data storage device that is made up of a flexible, round plastic disk encased in a hard plastic case. Most PC floppy disks are 3.5 inches in size and store 1.44 megabytes or 2.88 megabytes of information.

Folder A location on your disk where related files are stored.

Font A complete set of characters that share a specific typeface or appearance. A variety of fonts have been designed since the beginning of the written word. Most word-processing programs will allow you to pick the typeface that you prefer. You can also change fonts within your document if you wish. (See *Typeface.*)

Format bar A bar consisting of buttons and text options that allow you to format the characters in a document. It is usually found under the toolbar.

Formatting The process of setting up the font specifications, page layout, and design information for a document.

Function key A set of keys at the top of the keyboard that can be programmed to give specific commands or perform certain tasks. These keys are usually labeled F1 through F12.

Gigabyte 1,024 megabytes. The abbreviation for this is GB.

Graphical User Interface (GUI) This is pronounce "gooey" and refers to a method that allows computer users to point to icons or pictures on the screen in order to select files and give commands. It is the Microsoft Windows approach toward making the computer easier to use. Before this system was developed, PC users had to type a long list of characters in order to give each command. Apple Computers developed this easy interface and has always used it.

Hard disk The main storage area for data inside the computer.

Hard disk drive The device that is actually used to store the data and programs in the computer. It consists of sets of magnetically coated disks, called platters, that are stored vertically and rotate up to 3600 rpm. The unit is self-contained and sealed. Storage space on typical hard disk drives now tops 6 to 13 gigabytes and this continues to grow. (Note: the terms hard disk, hard disk drive, and hard drive are used interchangeably.)

Hardware A term referring to all the machinery or physical parts of the computer system.

Highlighting A way of marking text or information so that you can make changes to these sections of information when you give the next command. A highlighted section of text appears in contrasting color. Once something is highlighted, it can be cut, pasted, copied, or formatted.

Home page The initial starting page for a World Wide Web site. This page will usually provide an index and links to other pages on the site or to related information on other sites.

Hover To place the cursor over an icon for a short period of time. When this is done, a box will drop down that describes the function of the icon.

Hypertext Markup Language (HTML) A standardized language used to create pages on the World Wide Web. This language allows browsers to connect or link different pages to each Web site. This is not a "language" you will need to learn, it is just useful to know what the letters mean.

Icon A small picture that represents something such as files, folders, programs, commands, etc. Pointing the cursor at the picture and pressing the left mouse button gives the computer user access to them.

Inactive window The operating system or the application you are using might display several windows. All of these are "inactive" except for the window with the blue title bar and the cursor. (This is the "active" window.) An inactive window becomes active if you point the cursor somewhere in the window and press the left mouse button (click).

Insertion point A blinking vertical line or blinking I-beam cursor that indicates where the next character will appear when you type your next bit of text. It basically is a marker that says, "you are here."

Internet The largest computer network in the world. This is a "network of networks" that allows computer users to communicate with each other around the world using e-mail, the World Wide Web, etc. (See Chapter 4.)

Internet Service Provider (ISP) A company or service that connects the individual computer user to the Internet. A fee is usually charged for this service.

Keyboard The set of keys that look like a typewriter and are used to input text, data, and commands into the computer.

Keyboard commands A way of giving menu commands using the keyboard instead of the mouse. (See Appendix B.)

Keyboard shortcuts (See *Keyboard commands.*)

Key combinations (See *Keyboard commands.*)

LAN (See *Local Area Network.*)

Link A way of moving from one bit of information (a word, phrase, or idea) to another within a hypertext document. This information can be in the same or different Internet sites and is accessed through a Web browser. Links are easy to recognize because they are written in blue. The cursor changes to look like a hand when positioned over a link.

Local Area Network (LAN) A group of computers in the same area or place (such as an office) that are all connected. The purpose of a LAN is for people to share files and resources.

Log on (or Log in) To connect to an Internet Service Provider or some other network by entering an identification name or number and password. This is also known as "signing on."

Log off (or Log out) To disconnect from an Internet Service Provider or computer network by sending a message to terminate the connection. This is also known as "signing off."

Maximize/Restore button A button on the top right side of the title bar that increases the size of a window so that it fills the screen. When the window is already full size, clicking on the same button (which now looks like two overlapping windows) will restore the window to its original size.

Megabyte 1024 kilobytes or more than a million bytes. The abbreviation is MB and is pronounced "meg."

Megahertz A measurement of the speed at which a processor works. It is one million cycles per second, and the abbreviation is MHz.

Memory The place where data and programs are kept while they are in use. This is where all processing takes place. Later the information is stored on disks. There are two types of memory. RAM, or random-access memory, allows one to read and write information; data can be changed. Another type of information is ROM or read-only memory. This is information that cannot be changed and is usually used to start and program your computer.

Menu A list of commands that are available in the program with which you are working. By selecting options from the menus, you tell the computer what you want it to do. There are four main types of menus: menu bars, pull-down menus, sub-menus, and context menus.

Menu bar The row of words on the second line of a window just below the title bar. These words or names correspond to pull-down menus that allow you to perform different commands.

Microsoft Windows® The operating system used by most PCs. This is the system that simplifies how the computer works so that it manages applications, files, folders, disks, etc. in a "user-friendly" way. In the past, PCs used a complicated system of characters to issue all the instructions to the programs. Windows is a graphical operating system that uses icons and pull-down menus to give commands. (See *Graphical User Interface.*)

Minimize button A button on the top right side of the title bar that reduces an active window to an icon on the taskbar. In this way the application is ready to be opened again, but it is removed from view.

Modem A piece of electronic hardware that allows a computer to exchange data with another computer over the telephone lines.

Monitor The piece of hardware that looks like a television and displays information on a screen.

Motherboard The main circuit board in your computer. It holds the chips that are the central processing unit, memory, etc.

Mouse A device used for pointing on screen that lets you give commands and select items. A mouse usually has at least two buttons on the top that are pressed once or twice to select and activate commands.

Mouse pointer An icon that is either an arrow, a vertical line, a hand, etc. that is controlled by the movement of the mouse. It indicates where you are on the screen or in a window. The pointer allows you to select objects with which you want to work. Another word for the mouse pointer is "cursor."

"My Computer" icon An icon that sits on the upper left side of the desktop screen. When opened, it is used for file management and to get access to system tools.

Network Two or more computers that are connected for the purpose of sharing files, folders, programs, printers, and other resources.

Newsgroup A group of individuals on the Internet that are devoted to discussing a particular topic. Messages are "posted" electronically on a "bulletin board" so that others in the group can read and respond.

OCR (Optical Character Recognition) Software that takes an optically scanned image and converts it into letters and characters that can be recognized and used in text files by the computer.

Off-line 1) Hardware, such as a printer, that is not in "ready" mode and so is not available for use. 2) The term used when you are not connected to the Internet.

"OK" button An element in the dialog box that allows you to confirm a task. It also can take you to the next level of a program. Often you can press the "Enter" key instead of clicking on the "OK" button.

On-line 1) Hardware, such as a printer or a modem, that is ready to operate and is connected to a computer. 2) The term used when you are connected to the Internet.

On-line service A service that provides Internet connection and service to its subscribers through a modem.

Operating system Software that runs your computer and controls programs and hardware. Windows® 98 is an operating system. (See *Microsoft Windows.*)

Option buttons Small circles that are used in dialog boxes to allow you to make a single choice. When only one choice is possible you have the option of clicking this button to turn it on (button is black) or off (button is white).

Path A way of representing a directory or file that shows the location of the item in terms of the computer's filing system. It is a map that

173

names the drive, folders, and files in which the item is located.

PC   The acronym for "personal computer." It usually refers to a computer with a Windows operating system.

Pentium   A type of processor that was created by a company called Intel®. Currently there are several generations of this processor, including Pentium® II and Pentium® III.

Peripheral   The term for hardware, such as a printer, that is used with a computer.

Personal Computer   (See *PC.*)

Pointer   (See *Mouse pointer.*)

Port   A "socket" that allows you to connect hardware that is outside the computer to a circuit board within the computer. The circuit board then connects to the Central Processing Unit.

Processor   (See *CPU.*)

Program   A set of instructions that tell the computer what to do and how to do it. Programs are software.

Program buttons   Buttons that sit on the taskbar to show which programs and folders are "open."

Public domain software   Software that is not copyrighted, is freely distributed, and can be used or copied by anyone. Other names for this software are "freeware" and "shareware." It is most commonly available over the Internet.

Pull-down menu   A hidden, vertical menu that is opened with the menu bar. (The bar at the top of each window just below the title bar.) It allows you to access commands and features of that particular program.

Radio buttons (See *Option buttons.*)

RAM (See *Memory.*)

Random Access Memory (See *Memory.*)

Reboot To turn off the computer, start it again, and reload the operating system. This procedure is usually performed when the computer freezes or crashes, or after some new software is installed. Most computers have a "Reset" button that will restart the computer without turning off the power. Another way to reboot is to press the "Ctrl," "Alt," and "Delete" keys simultaneously (Ctrl+Alt+Del), or to go to "Shut Down" on the "Start" menu.

Recycle bin Your wastepaper basket. It holds all the data that you have deleted. It is visible on the desktop as an icon that looks like its namesake. As with all icons, if you double-click on this icon, it will open and you can view the contents. If you "empty" the recycle bin, all the information is gone permanently.

Restart An option in the dialog box from the "Shut Down" window of the "Start" menu. It is another way of rebooting the computer. (See *Reboot.*)

Restore (See *Maximize/Restore* button.)

Save A command that records or transfers your data onto the computer's hard disk for permanent storage. As you enter information it is placed into the computer's memory. Depending on the program you are using, it will be lost if there is a power failure, the computer crashes, there is a program error, or you turn off the machine. If you are using Microsoft Word®, it is very important to save your work every few minutes onto the hard disk or to change your settings to create an automatic backup file. Some programs, WordPerfect® and Quicken® among them, do save automatically. You should also save information on a floppy disk or zip disk every few days as an additional backup, no matter which program you are using.

Scanner A piece of hardware (peripheral) that lets you copy an image into the computer by changing the optical information to digital information.

Scroll bar A vertical or horizontal bar that appears on the right side and at the bottom of a window when there is more information in the window than can be seen at one time. It allows you to move down or over by clicking and holding down the appropriate arrow buttons in order to see the rest of the information. A small box within the bar shows you your relative position in respect to the information in the window.

SCSI An acronym for "small computer system interface" pronounced "scuzzy." Its purpose is to connect several pieces of hardware to your computer while only using one port.

Search engines Companies that use sophisticated software to find information on the Internet for computer users. Examples are www.Yahoo.com, www.lycos.com, and www.excite.com.

Select To choose an item on a menu or to highlight something. The result is that some action will take place with the next command you give.

Serial port The connector or socket that is used to attach or plug input and output peripherals such as a mouse or a modem to the computer.

Server A computer that provides files, data and other services to a network of computers. These other computers are called clients.

Shareware Software that is provided over the Internet free of charge for a trial period. If you continue to use the program you are asked to pay a fee. (See *Public domain software.*)

Shortcut A special icon that points to or represents another program, folder, file, etc., that is still in its original location on the hard drive. The icon sits on your desktop and allows you quick access to the program or information without taking up extra space. You can recognize these special icons by the little arrow in their lower left corner.

Shortcut keys Keys or combinations of keys that are used to give commands. They provide another way of asking the computer to perform some action when you do not want to use the mouse pointer to select and click a command from a menu or icon. Using shortcut keys is usually a faster way to give a command. (See *Keyboard commands* and *Function keys.*)

Shut down The proper way to turn off the computer and cut off its power supply. On the "Start" menu, the bottom option is "Shut Down." Opening that operation produces a "Shut Down" window and dialog box that gives several options including "Shut Down," "Restart," and "Standby." If you select the "Shut Down" button, the computer is turned off.

Software The term that is used to describe programs, operating systems, applications, etc. Basically if it is visible and a piece of equipment, it is hardware. If it is invisible and coded information that runs the computer, it is software.

Sound board (sound card) A circuit board that changes program instructions into high-quality sound. Most programs today are multimedia and take advantage of a sound board. Sound boards also make it possible for you to listen to your favorite audio CD while you work at your computer.

"Start" button A button on the extreme left side of the gray taskbar. By clicking on this button, the "Start" menu is opened.

"Start" menu A menu used to start programs, open folders and files, activate the help system, access the control panel to change settings, and much more. (See *"Start" button.*)

Startup disk A floppy disk or CD that holds all the operating system information. This is used to reboot your computer if the hard disk malfunctions.

Status bar The bar at the bottom of a window that gives you information that is related to the task or application with which you are working. In a word-processing program, the status bar tells you on what page you are typing, along with total number of pages of your document, and the line and column of your insertion point.

Surfing To browse the Internet. To surf means to move from one topic of interest to another while you are connected to the World Wide Web. Some people will spend hours going from one link to another. (See Appendix F.)

Surge protector A device used to regulate the electrical power that goes into the computer. It prevents electrical spikes or surges from damaging the computer. It is plugged into the electrical outlet, and the power cord of the computer is plugged into the surge protector.

System board (See *Motherboard.*)

"System" icon The icon on the far left corner of the title bar of each window. It opens a "System" menu that allows you to change features of the window such as moving, resizing, or closing the window.

"System" menu (See *"System" icon.*)

System unit The piece of hardware that looks like a box and holds all the circuit boards, disk drives, etc. that are the "inner workings" of the desktop computer. (See *Tower.*)

Tab This is found in dialog boxes and is similar to the tabs on folders that you keep in your filing cabinet. Just as with your files, these tabs are labeled. When selected they give a number of options corresponding to the name of that folder.

"Tab" key When using a word-processing program, this key inserts tabs just as it does on a typewriter. When using other applications, where it is necessary to fill-in data, this key moves the cursor from one "field" to the next. For example, when sending e-mail via

America Online, you can use the "Tab" key to move from the field "Send to" to the field "Subject" to the field where you enter your message. It is easier than pointing the cursor to a field and clicking.

Taskbar The horizontal bar running along the top or bottom of a window. It lets you know what programs are open on your desktop (even if they are not visible to you). You can use the taskbar to switch from one program to another by clicking on the button of the application you wish to use. Using these task buttons is much easier than going to pull-down menus. The taskbar also has the "Start" button and a clock.

Task button (See *Taskbar.*)

Title bar The horizontal bar at the top of each window that contains the name of the window (such as the application or file name) on which you are working. It also shows the minimize button, the maximize button, and the close button. When a window is active, the title bar is blue with white letters.

Toolbar The horizontal bar of buttons that is usually just below the title bar and menu bar. These are command buttons and each icon represents the most frequently used tasks. For some people, it is easier to point the cursor on one of these icons and click rather than using a pull-down menu or key command.

Tower A piece of hardware that holds the "brains" of the computer in a vertical case that usually sits on the floor. This is where everything is "plugged-in." The tower holds the drives, expansion slots, peripheral connections, and power connection. As towers become smaller, they often fit easily on your computer table or desk.

Trail A shadowed image of your mouse pointer that leaves a brief impression of where your mouse pointer is moving. This is a very helpful feature that you can add as an option on your mouse controller. It makes it much easier to find and see the mouse pointer.
Type size This is a measurement that tells the height of a font. It is

traditionally measured in "points." The type size that you are using in a text document is shown on the left side of the format bar.

Type style This refers to the effects that you can use to change the appearance of your text such as **bold**, *italic*, and underline. Either the button in the middle of the format bar or key commands are used to change type style.

Typeface The common design characteristics of a group of letters, numbers and symbols. The typeface is also known as the font, and you can see which one you are using in a text document by looking at the left side of the format bar. (See *Font*.)

URL (Universal Resource Locator) Another term for an address on the Internet. It is a series of characters that connect you to a specific site on the World Wide Web.

USB (Universal Serial Bus) The standard type of connection or interface between the different peripherals, such as the mouse and keyboard, and the computer. USBs allow you to plug in hardware and use it right away without rebooting.

Virus Software that is designed to damage your computer or files without your knowledge. Sometimes viruses are simple pranks and sometimes they are meant to destroy entire systems. Viruses are usually passed from one program or file to another through "infected" floppy disks you may receive, or by downloading something off the Internet that may be tainted. Some viruses can wipe out all the information stored on a hard disk. This is the reason you should back up your data on floppy disks or zip disks. In addition you can install antivirus software that will scan everything coming into your computer.

Web (See *World Wide Web.*)

Web browser (See *Browser.*)

Window The rectangle on your screen that shows a program or application and the data, file, or folder on which you are working. You can have several windows visible and open on your desktop simultaneously. However, only one window at a time is active.

Windows This refers to the operating system of your computer (as in Windows® 98) that was developed by the company called Microsoft®. (See *Operating System* and *Microsoft Windows®.*)

Word-processing software A program or application that allows you to use the computer as a typewriter. It manages text so that you can write, format, edit, and store documents. Examples of word-processing programs include Microsoft Word® and Corel's WordPerfect®.

World Wide Web A portion of the Internet that connects graphical and multimedia information (words, pictures, video, and sound). On the Web you can move from one site to another with the aid of a browser. (See *Internet, Browser, Link.*)

WYSIWYG An acronym for "what you see is what you get." It is pronounced "wizzy-wig." Programs that can show you on the screen exactly how they will look when printed out are called wysiwyg.

Zip disk (See *Zip drive.*)

Zip drive A disk drive that uses disks that are physically similar in size to floppy disks but hold much more data. A zip disk can store 100 megabytes of data.

I Index

Figures are indicated by an italicized *f* following the page number where the figure appears.

Backspace key, 9*f*
    correcting typing errors, 69
    highlighting and, 26–27
Barnes and Noble on the web, 56
beeping by computer, 95. *See also* binging
bifocals and computers, 157
binging by computer, 136–137
blank piece of paper, 77
blank screen, 134
Blue Mountain Cards on the web, 56, 151
bold/italicized/underlined, 72–74, 73*f*, 123, 139–140, 145
bolding, 73*f*
bookmarks, 54. *See* also Set My Places (AOL)
books, computer, 90, 138, 144
booting, 95
bottom of the window, 140
break from sitting at computer, 156
brokerage statement, 52, 53
browser, 161
    forward/back, 50*f*, 56
bundled software, 81
button configuration, mouse, 27*f*
buttons, 46, 162
buying online, 150

C drive, 37*f*, 162
    crashing, 18
cancel/OK, 43, 98. *See also* "Esc" key
capital letters, 139
caps lock key, 139
card games, computer, 60–62. *See also* Solitaire
cards, electronic greeting, 56, 151. *See also* Blue Mountain
CBS on the web, 56
CDs (compact disks), 81–84
    Encarta Encyclopedia, 82
    listening to, 130–131*f*
    loading and unloading, 84
    music and games, 84
    safety of, 84
CD-ROM. *See* Glossary
chair height and your computer, 155
changing settings in Control Panel, 97–98. *See also* Control Panel
click, left mouse button, standard, 21, 135
click, right mouse button, 21, 141

OK/Cancel, 43, 98, 173. *See also* buttons, esc key, enter key
online services. *See* AOL, Internet Service Providers
opening windows, 21–22, 100
operating system, 173
options, Solitaire, 61–62
outlet, grounded, 93

page numbers, bottom of screen, 140
parts of e-mail addresses, 47
pasting, cutting and, 75
PC, 174
physical health and your computer, 155–156
pointer. *See* mouse
ports, 2–93
power cord, monitor, 92
power symbol, 95
practicing computer skills, 59–62
preferences, setting, 7
Pentium, 174
preview, print, 125
previous page, 56
print preview, 125
printers
    cable for, 6
    connecting to tower, 92–94
    icon on toolbar, 126*f*
    installing/connecting, 93–94
    manufacturer and model, 94
printing, 75, 120
    documents, 125–126*f*
programs
    access to, 86
    active windows of, 137
    opening, 100
pull down menu, 174. *See also* drop down menu

questions, writing down, 13
Quicken (software), 52
Quotes (AOL), 50*f*, 52, 113

rebooting computer, 96, 175. *See also* restarting computer
recycle bin, 136, 175
red underlining, Microsoft Word, 69. *See also* Spell Check
replying to e-mail, 41–43, 105. *See also* e-mail
reset button, 142
resizing windows, 101
restarting computer, 18, 86–88, 87*f*, 88*f*, 96*f*, 115–116*f*
    how to, 96*f*
    need for, 116
    Start Menu, 86*f*, 87*f*, 114
return key. *See* Enter key
reverse typing mistake. *See* undo
right mouse button, 21, 141

Save As, 77–79, 78*f*, 121*f*
saving your work, 64, 77–80, 121*f*–122*f*, 127, 138
scissors icon, 138
screen saver, 141
screen, blank, 134
scrolling
    definition of, 26
    down or over, 101–102, 103*f*
    scroll bars, 82, 83*f*, 176
search engines, 57, 146, 176
search/find in *Encarta*, 82
secure site, 150
select. *See* highlighting
send
    e-mail, 42–44, 105, 107–109
    e-mail to more than one person, 44. *See also* group send
    e-mail later (AOL), 43, 108–109*f*
    now, 42*f*
Send Now (AOL), shaded, 108
Send To box (AOL), 42, 105, 108
Set My Places (AOL), 50*f*. *See also* bookmarks
setting up an account with an ISP, 46
setting up computer, 5–7
    hiring someone, 8
Settings, 7
    changing, 97–98, 99*f*
    Control Panel, 88–90, 89*f*
shaded
    desktop, 87, 115
    icons, 109, 134

Golden Mouse Award

This "Golden Mouse" certificate has been awarded to PC Master,

_____

[your name]

in recognition of completion of your "first week with your new PC" spent comprehending and accomplishing the skills of diligent unboxing, complicated machinery set-up, and mastering of software, keyboard keys, computer games, email correspondence with friends and family, Internet surfing, CD listening, and generally "getting connected" to the new world of personal computing.

Officially awarded this _____ day of _____month in the year of _____,

Authorized by

_____

Pamela R. Lessing, "First Week" Counselor